Marcus Bleecker

DUMBO

COLLECTED STORIES

Contents

COLLECTED STORIES

DUMBO

THIS TIME IT'S DIFFERENT

WELL, I'M TOSSED OUT. NOT LIKE BEFORE, THIS TIME IT'S DIFFERENT, AND I KNOW THAT BECAUSE SHE SAID SO. She told me this time it's different and that becomes clear when there's talk of keys. That lets me know that it's different, because the other times tempers flared and questions hung unanswered about touring and band rehearsals and not being around, not being available emotionally or being emotionally unavailable. Those other times there's crying but there's never been talk of keys and moving my stuff out. This time, however, that's what she says. She tells me that I need to give her my keys and I need to move my stuff out, and my heart burns but not like other times. Other times my heart burned, but there was never talk of keys and moving my stuff out. But, that's what was said and she tells me to gather my stuff and give her my keys, and then I hear footsteps on the stairs and that lady Vernice comes down the stairs and I'm like what the heck is she doing here, and I'm told that she's here for support, and Vernice puts a hand on Monica's shoulder to show me that that's the case, that she's here for support, then she says something about giving her my keys. I want to protest but no words come, they don't come and that's another reason why I know that this time it's different.

It's been three years since I met that lady Monica and we've had some really good times. I remember some of those times but those memories won't stick when I think of them, they just keep disappearing when I try to think of them and are replaced by that burning feeling that's in the middle of my chest because this time it's different. I try to take my keys off my little ring of keys and realize my hands are shaking and they don't even look like my hands, and then I'm thinking about moving back into my apartment which is a total dump and leaving this fine apartment that's plush and has furniture from Pottery Barn, and my apartment that has tattered furniture that's ratty and has stains on it.

This is what's happening and there doesn't seem to be anything I can do about it.

We had some fine times. But recently it hasn't been so fine and that's what happens. When you first meet it's all exciting, and being in a band and touring and playing gigs are exciting. When you are introduced to her friends it's he's in this band and he's touring and what kind of music is it and the band is awesome and all that, but then when the gigs don't pay so much and you still don't have a deal or the deal is a dud or the manager is a chump that clouds the excitement, then it becomes how many times a week do you have to rehearse and then you're not going to be here for my birthday because you're doing a show at some frat house at Hobart College and then it becomes a pain in the ass and you're called emotionally unavailable and I'm not blaming anyone, it's just the way it is and that's why I'm asked to turn in the keys and move out of this plush apartment on a beautiful tree-lined street in Brooklyn Heights, and I have to move back into my dump in Dumbo.

That's what's going to happen and there doesn't seem to be anything I can do about it. I walk down the spiral staircase that leads to the ground floor of this sweet walkup apartment building and there's a guy hovering around in the lobby, and upon hearing me he goes inside his apartment that is off the ground floor and closes his door and locks it and I'm thinking that maybe he's the one who has been stealing our *New York Times*. And It doesn't really matter anymore because this is probably the last time I'll descend these stairs. Everything is going to be different.

I walk home and it's one of those walks where you notice all the happy couples and people holding hands and kissing and it seems like I've never seen this amount of affection on the street before but I do and it all just makes me know that this time it's different because I've never seen anything like this.

I go into my building in Dumbo and the walk up the musty stinky stairs leads me into my apartment and I didn't mind this place so much when I didn't have to sleep here but now I do and the place feels awful. There's a ton of stuff all over my bed because I haven't slept here in years but now I'm going to be sleeping here in this dump and I don't have the sweet apartment to sleep in and this makes me realize that this time it's different.

THE HOVEL

MY BROTHER DECLARES THAT HE REFUSES TO TURN THIRTY AND BE LIVING IN OUR APARTMENT. I didn't ask him about this, but I guess he was thinking about it, because he just blurts it out of nowhere, and I know he expects me to say something, or challenge him or whatever, but I just laugh because it's kind of funny, because he's a candidate for a doctorate degree from The University of California at Santa Cruz, and has a master's degree from The University of Washington at Seattle, and an engineering degree from Cornell University, and he lives in a closet in Brooklyn, with bars on the window, and sleeps in a bunk bed that he bought at a children's furniture shop, and it's like six inches from the ceiling, so if he wakes up too quick, he slams his face on the ceiling that's right above his head. He's all embarrassed to bring people back to our flat because he knows they'll be like, why are you living in a closet?

I ask him, why thirty? Because I want to get him revved up about it, and he tells me he can't be living like this. I can tell he's been thinking about this and it bothers him, and he tells me something about being a grown man or whatever, and it just makes me laugh harder, and then I remember that I'm just a year and change behind him, so my laugh tapers off a bit because I'm also thinking maybe I should be getting my life together too, and be worrying about turning thirty and living in a dump and everything, but it's a little different, because I play drums in this band so it's kind of not as bad, I guess.

Two years ago I found this apartment when I said I'd play drums for a man named Gideon. He had a band called "The Blissful Kissful," and lived on the top floor of this three-level walk-up apartment in DUMBO ("down under the Manhattan Bridge overpass"). Gideon told me no one lived in the other two apartments. The landlord and his business partner used the flats to have liaisons with their mistresses. That explained the floor-to-ceiling mirrors in the front part of the flat and the bedroom. After I played a few shows for Gideon, he said he'd talk to the landlord about one of the apartments, because I needed a place to stay. Then he told me to call this lady named Connie to inquire about the flat. Connie told me she'd rent the second floor to me for two-hundred-fifty bucks a month, which was nothing, and was all I could afford anyway, because I made five-and-a-quarter an hour working at Tower Records. The place was a dump, but it had running water, and heat, and my band could play until all hours of the night, because no one lived nearby.

A year or so later my brother moved in, because he'd just arrived in New York City and needed a place to live. When I led him through the apartment and showed him the room in the back that this man named Tom used to live in, he told me to take the back room, and I made a sound as if to say, "Yeah, right." My brother stepped into his proposed room and peered through the filthy window with bars on it that led out onto the fire escape and down to the back of this joint called Los Papi's, which is a Spanish food place with rice and beans and whatnot.

The only thing we cooked in the apartment was hot water for our coffee press or canned soup, because this one time I poured breakfast flakes into a bowl and a dead mouse came out, so we tried to starve the mice by keeping food out of the apartment. In addition to the mice we also had water bugs the size of D batteries, and you'd have to run hot water into the shower for a minute or two, so you could wake the fuckers up, 'cause they'd come outta the drain and climb up your naked leg and everything.

Water bugs suck, and it's hard to see them, because they're brown, and the floor is brown and the couch is brown and when you do find them, and try to stomp on them, you realize they are big and nasty and look like pitted dates, and they sometimes just start flapping their wings and you're like, I didn't know this fucker could fly, and it's disconcerting and disturbing and demonic because the fucker is like flying in your face and it can't see shit and just flies wherever, whenever, and you swat at anything to get it away and you knock over a bunch of shit onto the floor and it's a pain in the ass, especially when it's like three in the morning and you just wanted to take a leak and it's turned into this whole battle in the living room, and your brother is moaning from the back room like, what the fuck is going on? And he comes around the corner in his skivvies and is shielding his pinched, bloodshot eyes from the light, and you tell him it's a water bug, and he's like, did you kill it? And I tell him no.

I ask that lady Connie if there's something we can do about the mice because it's turned into a situation where we tried to starve them out, but I keep finding these black pebbly droppings in the cabinets and on the table and on the bathroom floor and whatnot, and it sucks, and they're quite persistent, these mice in Brooklyn. That restaurant downstairs, Los Papi's, keeps their garbage and shit out in the alleyway beneath my brother's window and the smell is vile and rancid because they got stuff on their menu like tripe, and pig's snout and ears and tongue, and their garbage sits out in the alley all night and I can only imagine the feast the mice and rats and water bugs are having, and then they have babies and it's winter and it's cold and they figure they'll come up in my place to burrow after they eat, because it's warm and whatnot.

Connie asks me if I tried getting traps for the mice, and I tell her no. I go to this bodega and they have these wood traps with the metal bar that the Spanish guy tells me will snap their necks in half, and when I ask him if they work, he says yes. So I buy a three-pack and Gideon tells me to put peanut butter on the end of the trap, so I do. I slide one trap under the couch, put one on the kitchen floor, and another under the television in the middle room, and when I look under the couch there's all kinds of black pebbly things and I realize it's droppings from the mice and I'm disturbed because someone told me you can get sick with mold spores in your lungs from inhaling mice droppings, but I'm not as disturbed as I would be if they were bigger droppings, because then I'd be wondering if I had rats, and those fuckers bite, which would suck because you'd have to go to the hospital and get a whole mess of shots in your stomach, I've heard.

Anyway, something has to happen because I don't really sleep anymore, especially after this one man named Darryl told me that he found a mouse inside his pillow at his apartment because they like being in the stuffing and whatnot, and it reminds me of this kid, Kevin, who I knew when I was growing up who kept mice and hamsters in metal cages in his house, and they'd be all burrowed in this hay crap that looks like the stuffing of pillows and they'd be crapping in there and peeing and everything, and they'd be all white with red eyes and nasty looking, and Kevin would be like, pick it up, and I'd be like, no, and he'd put the little fucker on me and laugh, and it'd be this big joke because I'm all freaked out with this little fucker grabbing onto me with these little claws that would stick to my skin and it's nasty, especially when his kid sister turns the darn thing over in my hand and says, it's a boy, see? and she's spreading open the little fucker's groin area and it's got this little pink thing sticking out and it's all moist-looking and I'm like, who the fuck cares?, and then it pees on me and I swat the fucker to the floor, and that kid Kevin would be all upset because the mouse scampered under a bed or something and his sister would be crying to high hell and back, and Kevin would be searching the room, calling the little fucker's name like, that's gonna do anything, and his mom would come in all salty and whatnot and be looking for the mouse and be like glaring at you, and you'd just want to go home, but you said you'd sleep over and now it's too late to call your parents and tell them to come get you, and then you have to go to bed in a sleeping bag on the floor, and the mouse is still missing and you don't give a fuck, as long as that little fucker doesn't crawl into your sleeping bag in the middle of the night and try and burrow in the stuffing.

I'm always waking up in the middle of the night and flicking the lights on in my bedroom because I think I feel something crawling on my leg or creeping into my pillow or something, especially after I found a water bug in my bed and beat the living shit out of it with a curled up phone book, and I imagine all his boys and the rest of his family plotting revenge.

I kick one of the traps out from under the kitchen table and the peanut butter is gone but there's no mouse in the trap and this really ticks me off because now the fucker is fed and he's probably all hopped up on peanut butter and thinks he knows where to have dinner now, and his boys are like, there's food on the second floor, and who knows what kinds of shit is making its way up into my flat.

This one lady named Anika tells me that I need to fill any holes in my walls with steel wool 'cause she says mice can't bite through steel wool, and I imagine their little nasty teeth biting through my breakfast cereal box and I look for holes in my walls or whatever and there's fucking holes in the walls and in the floor, and the fucking mice are having a goddamn field day.

This one morning I go to brush my teeth and there are mouse droppings in the sink and everything, and I nearly puke my bowels. I declare war because this is getting ridiculous and it's really got me pissed because I can't sleep and I can't eat in my own goddamn apartment, and one of those little fuckers was probably eating food remnants off my toothbrush and that's just plain out nasty, and at some point enough is enough.

The guys in my band come over to rehearse and they bring stapled-shut Styrofoam containers stuffed with greasy Chinese food that smells like ass, and they eat it in the living room, and I'm all on edge because I haven't slept, and there's food in the house and it stinks to high hell, and I know the mice are like, cool, 'cause they smell the food and they're probably all geared up to find greasy rice and lo mein and shit on the floor, so I'm all paranoid about food falling onto the floor, and my fears are confirmed when I go to take the trash out the following morning and I listen to the garbage bag and it's making all this racket and there's a goddamn mouse in the garbage bag having a fucking ball with the Chinese food.

This one lady tells me to get some glue traps, so I get a six-pack of these little dishes that smell like food or whatever and have glue on them so the mice will get stuck. Gideon tells me that they work, but mice sometimes get trapped and all freaked out and if their leg is stuck on the trap or their arm or something, they'll chew it off so they can be free, and the limb will eventually grow back, and I'm like fuck

Brooklyn and fuck living down by the water, because it sucks having this problem and not getting sleep and I'm thinking that maybe my brother is onto something and we should split this scene before he turns thirty.

I wake up in the middle of the night and there is all this flapping going on in the middle room and I flip the lights on and there's this fucking mouse in the glue trap freaking out and flapping around and everything and it's not a little mouse like that kid I knew had, it's big and long and has teeth and is dingy, dirty grey, and nasty from Brooklyn, and I'm like, now what the fuck do I do? Because I'm definitely not touching this fucker and it's still alive, so now what? I can hear my brother moaning from his closet because it's five in the morning and he's all pissy, so I pick up the broom and wind up to swat this fucker and it's like something that's alive and has blood and legs and eyes and shit, and I'm like you better nail it just once, so I wind up the broom, and this fucker is flapping all over the goddamn place like a fucking fish out of water and it gets more intense like it knows what the fuck I'm about to do and I wail down with the broom and slam the trap, and the fucker comes loose and scampers around and jumps up at me and it's too close and the broom is too long and the little fucker hits my naked leg and it's all disturbing and I swat and slam and dance out of the way, and the fucker takes another jump at me like he's pissed, and I knock it out of the way and it bounces off the couch, and the glue trap is stuck to the end of the broom, and the mouse just scampers somewhere under the couch and the broom goes flying into my drum set with all kinds of noise and cymbals crashing and whatnot, and my brother comes out of the back room in his skivvies all perturbed and is like, what the fuck's going on? And I tell him there was a fucking mouse in the glue trap, and he's like, did you kill it? And I tell him no.

My dad calls and tells me he wants to come over to take us to lunch and I'm like, why don't you just meet us somewhere? And he says he wants to see our flat and I'm not sure why. For starters our doorbell doesn't work and my pops has got no voice 'cause his vocal chords are messed up, so he's like out in front of our flat for way too long and it's a sketchy block so he's not in the best mood when I finally see him. I let him in and he climbs up the fucked-up staircase that smells like cat piss, and he comes inside. His eyes move across the exposed brick wall, the CD cases precariously piled on top of the stereo and television, the drum set that takes up half the room, the tattered Persian carpet that used to be in his living room, the guitar cases, amplifiers, cords, cables, wires, and microphone stands. He takes refuge on the couch that used to be his and is now all slumped and sad-looking because too many people crash on it, like that man Darryl did because his wife asked that he find a different place to live and so he asked us if he could maybe crash on our couch and it's like, what are you gonna say? So we tell him it's okay, but he's like six-foot-six and three hundred pounds and that couch didn't have a prayer, and will never be the same, and I remember this one time my brother comes out in the middle of the night to get some water or whatever and goes into the middle room to catch some television and forgets that that man Darryl is passed out on the couch, and Darryl has to wear this fucking oxygen mask and has a tank and everything because he's got that thing where you might die in your sleep because you stop breathing, and he scares the living shit out of my brother because it's dark as fuck, and Darryl is like this huge dude with dreads and a fucking space mask strapped to his head like he's out of some *Alien* movie, and my brother says he nearly shit himself.

Anyway, my dad calls our place a hovel and me and my brother crack up because he's all serious, with his hands folded in his lap and shaking his head and slumped in the fucked-up couch, and he says something about the Board of Health and he's wondering how we could live like this, and he says we're living like squatters and we crack up even more and he's probably thinking about all the money he spent on college and whatnot and we're living in this dump, and when he sees where my brother lives in that back closet with the bed he bought at a children's furniture shop and the bars on the dirty window and all, he's like you guys live in a hovel, and each time he says that word we laugh harder because he's right.

The Projects

I CALL THE AREA WE LIVE IN BEIRUT BECAUSE THERE'S BROKEN GLASS ON THE SIDEWALKS AND SMASHED CRACK VIALS AND DOG SHIT EVERYWHERE BECAUSE PEOPLE WALK THEIR DOGS DOWN OUR STREET AND THEY NEEDN'T BOTHER CLEANING UP AFTER THEIR CANINES BECAUSE THERE'S NO ONE TO SAY ANYTHING TO THEM, AND IF THERE WERE, WHAT THE HELL ARE YOU GOING TO SAY WHEN THERE'S DOG SHIT NEXT TO BROKEN WINE BOTTLES, AND THE STREET SPARKLES WITH BROKEN CRACK VIALS? No one cares about anything anyway except getting home without getting cold-jacked by some eleven-year-old hoods who ride around on those little bikes that are silver and pimped out, and they're eleven but all hard and cold and saying shit to you when you're just walking down the street minding your own business, and they got those face masks on and bandanas and everything, and have like ten dudes in their posse and they live in the worst projects in Brooklyn, which are like a block away from my flat. You can hear gunshots all through the night, and someone told me it's dudes on the rooftops practicing their aim, and that's just what I need to hear because you always see those breaking stories on the five o'clock news about some kid who was sleeping in his bed and then felt something warm and wet in the covers and it turns out a stray bullet busted through the wall and now he's got a hole in his torso or whatever.

Anyway, when you exit our train stop you have two choices: you can make a hard right and walk straight past the projects where there are usually people out on the corner carrying on and whatnot, or you can head straight down towards the water and it's dark as sin and the street lights barely work, and no one goes down there because if you wanted to jack somebody up or shoot illicit drugs into your veins it'd be like a no brainer because there's an abandoned parking lot on one side of the street and another one on the other side of the street, so if you yelled or whatever it'd be worthless. I go this way sometimes because dudes will usually say shit to you if you go the other way, and this way you have a pretty good chance of seeing no one, and if you do see someone, you walk out in the middle of the street and act like you're not well because this one man told me that that's what you do if you think you're about to get jacked up. He said you walk out in the middle of the street like you got mental difficulties and if it's looking like you're about to get jacked you stick your finger down your throat and let your bowels spill out because this man told me that'll scare them off. This one time this dude was following me and I was carrying my cymbal bag and he's trying to talk to me all normal but there's nothing normal about following someone to their flat at three in the morning and I just want him to leave me be, but he's not doing that, and he's all sweaty and beady-eyed like a starving crack head, and he tells me he used to play drums, which could very well be the case, but it's not what I want to talk about on a dark street at three in the morning with an abandoned parking lot on either side of the street and a blinking street light, and some dude following me, glaring at my cymbal bag like it's a big greasy crack vial. And then he asks me if I play in that band down the street and I'm like, yeah, and I'm thinking that sucks that he knows about the band because the last thing I need is some crack head hanging outside my apartment looking for some music gear to pawn. He starts telling me that he can get guitars and I'm like, great, and he tells me something about a Gibson Les Paul and I don't play guitar but I don't tell him that and then he goes on about how hungry he is and I give him a five-dollar bill because I need to be left alone, immediately. Then he tells me he's gonna pay me back, and I tell him I don't want him to pay me back, and I realize I'm fucked because now this dude's gonna be outside my place all the time fucking with me and trying to sell me shit and looking for shit to sell and whatnot, and I think of him again when I come home this one time on a Sunday morning and it's cold as fuck and there's this dog tied to the railing outside my flat and I'm like, who the fuck has tied their dog up outside my flat? And the fucker is carrying on and barking and snarling, and as I get closer I see that the damn thing is all mangy and its skin is ripped up and all raw and it's a pit bull and there's foam and shit in its jowls, and spittle flying every which way, and it's lunging at me and inadvertently choking itself cause it's tied to my railing and I'm like, for fuck's sake, and I'm thinking maybe that man Gideon knows something about this, like maybe one of his friends is upstairs and left his mangy pit bull outside, and it's fucked up because I can't get to the door without getting ripped apart by this mutt, and that pisses me off worse, so I call Gideon and he's like, yeah, there's a dog outside, and he tells me he doesn't know who put it there so I'm like, fuck, call the cops, and he says he already did, like, three hours ago and they still haven't come and it's a pretty good chance they won't because they got other shit to deal with like stabbings and rape and murder and whatnot, and it's just some poor dog that has probably been in one of them dog fights where assholes bet, and some jerk put it in front of my house and I'm thinking it's the crack head dude who followed me home that one night.

Anyway, this one time I'm deciding which way to go and it's like, six in the evening, so working folks are exiting the train and everyone is keeping to themselves and hurrying home from work, and I'm deciding which way to go, and this one lady looks over at me and she sort of smiles and turns away and she's heading up the way where most folks are going so I go the same way, up by the projects, and she turns again, and I'm trying to act like I'm not following her but it's pretty clear I'm trying to get in her business, and I feel all stupid because what are you supposed to say to someone who walks ahead of you and kind of smiles without sounding stupid or have her be like, back the fuck off, 'cause it's pretty rough in this neighborhood and I've seen ladies come out the train and be like, fuck off, to guys who try and get with them. So I move closer to her and she looks at me again, so I'm like, hi, and she says, hi, and it's like what do I say now? But she's like, you live over here? And I'm like, is she talking about the projects? So I say, yeah, but I live just down the street, and she's says, really? I tell her really, and then she allows me to walk with her a bit and she's studying me and trying to catch my vibe and it's pretty dark out and the dim street light doesn't help much but I can see enough to tell that this lady is fine and she's got a real nice face, and I'm thinking I'd like to see her sometime. Then she asks me, what's down the street? And I tell her, there is this one apartment building in the middle of the block next to this one Spanish place called Los Papi's, and she's like, really?

Like she had no idea there was anyone living back there, which isn't really that difficult to imagine. Anyway, we get to the corner and I need to make a left and she needs to make a right so I say something stupid like, see you later, and she says she wants to come see where I live sometime, and I'm getting that burning feeling on my face because it's only half a block since I've known this lady but she's cool, and I give her my card, which is totally stupid and lame because my card says I'm a drummer, which is probably the stupidest thing you could put on a card because people are always saying shit about drummers being stupid and whatnot, but she says, you play drums? And she acts like she's all interested. Then she says she thought she heard music coming from down my street, and I'm like, yeah, probably it was my band, so she's looking at the card and says my name and then introduces herself and says her name, and we shake hands, and I say her name like I didn't hear it right 'cause it sounds funny and she's like, no, it's like Vanilla with a D, so I say what? And she tells me that that's how you say her name. So I say Donella like she tells me to say it. Then I say, see you later, and then she calls me that night.

That lady named Donella's apartment is really loud and there's people carrying on and screaming, and every couple of minutes someone gets on the other end of the line and Donella yells at them, and they go back and forth like that, and you can hear a television blaring and someone cooking and running the sink and whatnot, and she's all miffed and hollering and covering the phone with her hand or something, and this goes on every so often until she's like, I'll call you back, and she never does, until this one night my brother tells me this lady named Donella called and he says it wrong like Don-ella and he tells me she wants that I should call her back, so I call her and some guy answers the phone and says, who dis? And I'm like, what? And he's like, who dis? So I hang up and I'm feeling all stupid, so I call back again, and this time I ask for that lady who called and he yells her name all loud and the way he says it is how you're supposed to say it, so now I understand what she means when she says vanilla with a d. Donella picks up the other end of the phone and she's hollering with that man who picked up the phone, and she's covering the phone and it's all muffled until I hear a door slam and all kinds of fussing because she's got the phone pressed into her hand or something, and then she gets back on the phone and she's like, I want to come see your apartment, meet me on the corner. So I'm like, tonight? And she tells me she's stressed and needs to get out of her apartment, and I'm like, when?

And she's like, now, so I spray some bleach on the toilet and brush my teeth and make my bed.

I go to meet her on the corner near the projects and dudes are out acting wild, and this dude is clocking me and then walks over to where I'm standing and walks right by me and says some shit to me that I ignore and then keeps on saying shit and I'm all tense and like, I hate people starting shit with me, and then I turn and look at the dude and it's that lady I'm supposed to meet and she's all dressed differently like she's got all her hair up under a baseball cap, and she's got these big-ass glasses on and a big-ass trench coat and I hardly recognize her, and she tells me she's gotta dress like a boy so motherfuckers don't start shit with her, and I'm all thrown off but we go inside my apartment and she tells me she needs a hug, so I hug her, and she pulls out a twelve-inch steak knife from the front of her trousers and I'm thinking she's gonna stab me, but she tosses it on top of her trench coat and says something like, protection, so I know why she's carrying a big-ass steak knife.

She tells me her family is driving her nuts and I let her go on and tell me about her mom who she adores but wishes would stop smoking Newport cigarettes, and her out-of-control brother, and younger sister, who is fourteen and has a baby, and some other girl named Layshawn or La Wanda or something who is on drugs and is related to them, and stole stuff from their apartment like a television set and jewelry and whatnot, and how she had to get a lock put on her bedroom door, and her dad who is fucked up and in and out of jail, who tries to call her collect and she's tired of him and she's sick of her siblings and that lady who steals shit from her house, and she just wants to not get pregnant and finish college so she can get out of the projects and move somewhere nice, like Pennsylvania. I ask her if she's ever been to Pennsylvania and she's like, no. Then she asks if she can use the bathroom and I'm like okay, and I walk her back there and my brother is in his room and hears us but he doesn't bother coming out to say anything and I know he's too embarrassed to let people know that he lives in that closet in the back, and he's probably thinking who is this lady in his house and whatnot, and she goes into the narrow bathroom and I'm hoping a water bug doesn't come out and freak her out. Then I hear a loud crash and she tells me she stomped on a big-ass water bug like it's no big deal.

I have this little television in my bedroom and we watch that stupid movie called *When Harry Met Sally* and it's this romantic comedy and I feel all stupid watching it because it's a movie about couples that have been together a long time and relationships that are rocky, and it's a movie you shouldn't really be watching on a first date, especially with someone who has got mad problems, and Harry and Sally and their friends are moaning about being in love and out of love and whining about their relationships, and it's got nothing to do with the projects and it's a completely different world than what Donella knows, and then I steal a glance at her glazed eyes and I wonder if she's completely bored or thinking about smacking Meg Ryan in her whiny face, but she looks kind of into it and I wonder if this is what she thinks about when she thinks about Pennsylvania and just having regular everyday problems. Ten minutes into it I wish I could shut it off so I'm like, do you want a massage? And she looks at me all sideways and says sure, and just like that she pulls up her shirt and I'm like, cool, and she unhinges her bra and her tits are perfect and I wish I could turn the lights on and see them for real because the television light is all dim but I can see enough to know that they are round and just look perfect. Anyway, she lays down on her stomach and I rub oil on her back and try to be all good at it like I know what I'm doing when I don't, but she digs it anyway and next thing I know she's like asleep and I'm like, whatever, and I lay down next to her and pull the blanket over us and after a while she wakes up in a panic and tells me she's gotta go, and I tell her she should stay over because I don't want her to leave, and more importantly I am strongly opposed to walking her back down the street because it's midnight and dudes are for sure out on the corner looking to start shit and I know this because that man Gideon went down the street to get Chinese food late at night and got cold cocked in his eye and robbed by this kid who Gideon said looked like he was twelve. I can tell she's real apprehensive about staying over and whatnot, so I tell her I'll sleep in the other room on the couch and she's like no, and starts gathering her crap and I try and be all convincing and hold her hand and everything and I'm terrified to walk outside, especially with her, because if some dude gets to starting shit I'm gonna look like a chump because I'll cower like the wimp I am and the dude will be like ten years old, and that's just embarrassing. I get her to lie back down in the bed but she's uncomfortable and restless and keeps mumbling about how she can't stay over. She lets me kiss her and we carry on like this for a bit until I let my hand drop down and take hold of one of her butt cheeks in my palm and pull her closer, and she blurts out that she's not trying to get pregnant and I'm like what? And she's like you heard me and then she says it again, and I ask her why she's so obsessed with getting pregnant. I mean, we were fully clothed, and she tells me that her sister is fourteen and has a baby and her mom had her when she was sixteen and her cousin has two kids and is nineteen and none of them are ever gonna leave the projects because they got these kids, and something about state checks and welfare, and they can't have no man around and that's why she's paranoid about getting pregnant, and I assure her that we aren't going to get pregnant and she asks me how do I know? and I'm starting to think that maybe this isn't such a good idea, but that flesh between my legs has other plans so I roll her onto her back and start dry humping her and it's fine by me, and she seems to dig it as well. I don't know how long this went on for but at some point I had sufficient zipper burn on the under side of my penis and stopped this business and fell off to sleep.

In my dreams I was at the Community Park Pool of my youth, in Princeton, New Jersey. It was me, my sister, my brother, and our babysitter James, and I was on the high dive and everyone was like, jump! And I'm all scared and I want to go back down but there's someone climbing up the ladder behind me and they're like, jump! And I look down at my Speedo and I have a boner and everyone starts laughing and pointing so I jump and hit the water with a splash and go down, down, down and I'm swimming up and up and up and I'm not getting to the top and I'm holding my breath and it's running out, and wham! I wake up in the hovel with my heart beating like a tom-tom. My breath halts because I reach my hand down under my ass and it's warm and wet and the bed is soaked and I'm like fuck, and that lady is like asleep right next to me and I'm all embarrassed and I'm in a pool of urine and I'm trying not to move around too much because I don't want to wake her up and everything, and how do you explain peeing yourself when you're like old and shit?, and this doesn't happen often or anything but it has happened, but it's usually when I'm passed out drunk or something, like that time I was at my friend's parent's beach house and we got lit the fuck up over Fourth of July weekend and I woke up in the guest bed with soaked sheets, and the mattress was soaked with piss, and it was a mess, so I bundled up the lot of it and went out in the woods and buried the bundle of pissy sheets, then rifled through his mom's linen closet at four in the a.m. looking for bedding, and his mom comes out in the hallway and is like, what the heck is going on? And I'm like trying to play like I'm looking for the bathroom when I'm on the opposite side of the house from where my room is, and she's all suspicious and like, go back to bed, and then I have to give it a go later in the night and dig into the linen closet and find some bedding, but I get it back to the guest room and it's linens for a king-size bed and I'm in this little cot and I'm like fuck this, and I just pull a blanket over the bed and sort it out in the morning. Then the rest of the weekend I'm paranoid that his mom or someone will find the pissy sheets in the woods, so I dig in the woods myself and bury them better, and it's just stupid sometimes the things I get myself into.

Anyway, that lady named Donella who lives in the projects stirs awake and I pretend to be asleep and I'm like fuck's sake, this sucks, and there's no way she doesn't feel the piss-soaked bed because the both of us are sitting in a pool of urine and it's a futon so it's like this big pissy sponge and she starts fussing and gets out of the bed and is all moaning and carrying on but hush-like because she's trying to be quiet and not wake me up and then I get to thinking because of the way she's carrying on and fussing and being quiet that it was her who peed my bed, and then I feel embarrassed for her because she's all grown and I made her stay over because I didn't want to walk her down the street because I didn't want to get jacked up by an eleven-year-old thug on the corner, and now she's peed my bed and is all embarrassed and I'm trying to be still in the bed but my face is facing her and she can probably see my twitching eyelids that won't sit still, and my mouth is moving and I have to swallow and I try and make like I'm asleep, and she leaves the room and I'm like, did she split? I finally swallow and I'm piss-soaked and I confirm that it was her when I reach over to where she was sleeping and I thought my side of the bed was pissy but her side is like a goddamn lake bed, and then she comes back in the room all fussy and I close my eyes and lay back in the pissy bed and I can hear her ripping paper towels and it's sad and I feel bad for her and I'm lying in a pool of warm piss and it's absurd, and she shakes me awake and is all moaning and embarrassed and I'm like, it's all right, and she's like, I knew I shouldn't have stayed over, and I'm like, don't worry about it, and I'm trying to play like it's no big deal but my futon is going to smell like a cat box and that's that.

She promises me she's gonna buy me a new futon but I tell her no and she insists, and I'm like don't worry about it, and she's trying to soak up the piss with paper towels and we have them cheap-ass bodega paper towels that are good for nothing, and she is moaning, and I'm like in my skivvies and I look ridiculous because they are grey and my ass is a darker shade of grey because it's soaked with urine and she tells me that she needs to go get a hair dryer to dry out the pissy futon and she tells me she has to go home and get it, and I'm thinking that this type of shit must happen to her a lot because I would've never thought to use a hair dryer, and it sounds like she's done this before and then she leaves and I don't blame her when she never comes back.

That lady Donella never calls me again and I'm like whatever, and I'm not sure what to do about this pissy bed but I know it's gonna reek like hell and the mice would probably love a good pissy futon to burrow in, so I put it out on the street and the crack head dude is out there and he's like, you getting rid of it? And I'm like, it's no good, and he's like why? And I'm like, it's got piss all over it, and he looks at me like I did it, with his face all twisted up, and I don't care.

I go back inside the apartment and I tell my brother that maybe we should get cracking and go look at apartments, and he just looks at me like he's trying to figure out why I'm saying this and he rubs his nose and sniffles and asks me, when?
We walk down the street to get on the F train and we see that crack head dude lying down on my pissy futon and my brother recognizes my batik futon cover and is like, isn't that your bed? And I'm like, yeah, and my brother twists up his face and shakes his head and I can tell that now he's got some idea why I told him we should get cracking and go look at apartments.

THE NEW YORKER

THIS FRIEND OF MINE NAMED WILLIE HEARS THAT I'M SELLING MY CAR AND HE TELLS ME HE WANTS TO BUY IT BUT I'M NOT SO SURE I WANT TO SELL IT TO HIM. His name is actually Steve Williams but folks call him Willie and it suits him much better than Stevie. Anyway, my dad gets a new car every four years through his job and he has an option to buy the car, so he bought this car and he gets it all cheap, and then his idea is to turn around and sell it and maybe make a few bucks on the deal. So he did that, he bought the car and then got a new car through his job and he took the car that he bought and he gave it to me to use for a bit, like three or four months so I can have some wheels, and it's been about six months and my dad is like, sell the car, and it's kind of a tough thing because I like having the wheels, and he knows this and he knows he's going to have to bother me about it because he knows how I am. So he bothers me a bunch and he's like, sell it already, and so I take out this advertisement in the classified section of the local paper and people call and ask about the car and I tell them it's a Chrysler New Yorker, turbo, black with a brushed tan velour interior. I tell them it's got 112,000 miles on it and most people pause and repeat that figure back to me. They say, 112,000 like a question so I just tell them yes. And, okay, yes, I don't kick into a salesman pitch and I don't tell them how peppy the car is or that it's in great shape and never had any problems and whatnot because quite frankly I don't want to sell it.

Willie asks me how much I want for it and my dad told me the Blue Book value is five grand, so that's what I tell Willie and he says no problem and he tells me that he needs a few weeks to put the money together and I tell him, okay. When I tell my dad that I have someone, a friend, who wants to buy the car, he asks who and I tell him it's this guy named Willie and my dad doesn't say anything and the silence actually does say something and I'm wondering what shade of red his ears are turning, and then after a while my dad says something about just take care of it and I try and act like nothing could possibly go wrong and I tell him, of course, and my dad is silent and he's probably thinking about all the possible things that could go wrong, because with me, things do go wrong, especially with someone named Willie.

A few weeks pass and Willie tells me he's put together the money and he asks that I drive the car over to his flat so he can take a look at the vehicle, and there's this guy with him who Willie tells me is a mechanic and his name is Will. Will's hands are all grimy with black grease so I just nod to him and Will goes and pops open the hood and Willie adjusts his baggy maroon velour running pants and asks that I follow him inside. Willie's room is just that, a room, and he's got a duffel bag packed in the middle of the floor and that's really all there is in this room other than a bare mattress with what looks like a big coffee stain smack in the middle of it and when I think about it, it's probably not a coffee stain. He digs into his closet and pulls out a shoebox and flips the lid open and the blue Adidas shoebox is stuffed with money and a big Ziploc bag of pot. Willie hands me the box, so I take it and then I look at him and he's got this look on his face like he wants to say something but he forgot what it is he wanted to say. After a few moments of that look he tells me that I can count it, so I spill the money out onto the bare mattress, away from the coffee stain, and begin counting it. There are twenties, tens, and some dollar bills all natty and crinkled like they've been handled in a bunch of small time transactions by this one and that one and it's not a stretch because Willie is a small time pot dealer, maybe a little coke or ecstasy, it's how he makes a living. Anyway, Willie tells me that he's got a deal for me, and his hands are down the front of his running pants like he's fussing with his unit or something and I'm like what the fuck is that about, and I'm all distracted and I'm hoping this isn't one of them type deals where you need to shake on it because his hands are all up in his business. Willie tells me that it's a way that I could make some extra money and then he tells me that he couldn't put all of the money together but he has $2,700 and six ounces of weed, which he tells me is the hydroponic bud that sells for $600 an ounce, easy. He tells me this and then he says it again, easy, and now his smile is gone and there is a crease in between his eyebrows like he's concentrating on a serious math equation. I stop counting the money and I don't remember where I was anyway because of the hands on the crotch thing and the other thing about the sweet deal, and this isn't what was supposed to happen this particular day, but days be like that for me sometimes and I'm a bit thrown off and have no idea how much money I counted so I set my handful of cash back on the bare mattress, and I can feel the moisture gathering on my palms. I turn my blank gaze to the window and I can hear that man Will fussing with my dad's Turbo Chrysler New Yorker with the brushed velour interior and I'm thinking this is what my dad's silence was all about, because he knows how these things work and all the possible things that can go wrong with friends with names like Willie who want to buy your dad's car, and I'm wondering how he knows that that's how it goes down. I mean, I'd love to hear the stories of the folks that he knew, like Willie, who were straight bullshitters and were always into this, that, and the other thing and hustling and whatnot, and how did my dad know that this was going to happen even though he doesn't know Willie and how could he know that I would know that I shouldn't take the $2,700 and the six ounces of bud, but that I would, because I'd be thinking that I could sell four of the ounces and make a sick profit, and this is what Willie is telling me, that he's making me the sweetest deal on earth and he's telling me that it'd be silly to not jump at the chance, and he's trying to make me understand that he's doing me a favor and hooking me up, and I know what it is he's trying to do, I know the hustle, and he's telling me that he's leaving for Minneapolis in the morning and he could use the money and buy a plane ticket but he'd much rather buy the car from me and hook me up with the sweet deal.

I don't tell my dad that I sold the car because he's going to want the five grand right away. What I do is I start making phone calls to folks so I can unload the bud real quick, and once I put together the five grand I'll tell my dad it's a done deal and that'll be that. So I call my friend George who is this guy I know from high school and he smokes pot all the time and he's like, what's going on? And he asks me if I know anyone who might want to buy some weed and my heart does that burning thing that it does when stuff like this happens and I tell him that I don't know anyone who wants to buy any weed and he tells me that he's got the KGB, and I'm not sure what he's talking about and he tells me it's the kind green bud and I ask him how much he's selling it for and he tells me he's selling it for $400 an ounce and I'm like, really? And I'm trying to get a sense of how high-powered his weed is compared to my Willie weed, so I can gauge the worth of this bag of weed that sits on my bed inside a Ziploc baggie, and George tells me it's the killer bud. I ask George if that's the price, the going rate for the ounce of weed, and he tells me it's a good deal and my heart does that burning thing again.

I roll a joint of my Willie weed and I spark it and I let it burn for a bit and I smell the air and it doesn't smell bad, so I puff a bit and I only smoke a few hits because I want to make sure it's the kind green bud, the KGB. I get high but I'm not floored or nothing because I'm not all paranoid and I'm not thinking that I can't breathe or that my heart is beating too fast or something. Then the phone rings and the caller ID tells me it's my dad and my heart does that burning thing because this is just the way shit happens when you do stuff like this, when you get involved with folks like Willie who say they are going to buy your dad's Turbo Chrysler New Yorker with a brushed tan velour interior and instead give you some money and six ounces of weed and then you call your friend George and he tells you he's got the KGB for $400 an ounce. I make a few more phone calls and my friend Randy tells me he just got back from Amsterdam and he tells me they snuck back some hash oil inside his 35mm camera and he tells me that they smoked their asses off and he's going to decompress for a while, and he goes on and tells me other stuff like about the bars where you can order bud and mushrooms off a menu like you were in a restaurant and he tells me how it's no big deal there and he's telling me that I have to go, and then he says it again, he tells me I have to go. My heart does that thing again, that weird flutter thing, but it's not as intense as the first time, and Randy's going on about this, that, and the other thing and I mention to him that I have the KGB and he's like, what? So I tell him it's the kind green bud and he says, sweet, and then his voice is interrupted like someone is calling on his other line and he tells me he's got another call that he needs to take.

So now I'm thinking that maybe I should sit on the weed for a bit and just put together $2,300 somehow or maybe I should just undercut the market value of the bud and sell it at a basement price so I can get rid of it and get that $5,000 to my dad, and forget about the sick profit. So, I'm looking at this pile of cash, this $2,700 that's a rag-tag of twenties, tens, and dollar bills from all the small-time drug deals to this one and that one, and it's probably the most money I've ever seen in one place, and it smells like ink and I start to wondering where Willie is and I'm thinking he's on the road with that smile on his face and there's no way I can go back and tell him no way and take the car back, and I look at the license plates in the corner that I plucked off the car, the license plates that Willie asked me to leave on the car and he assured me he just needed them on until he could get his paperwork in order, and I'm pretty stupid, but that just seemed like the worst idea ever, so I took them off with a screwdriver that that man Will handed me after a long pause.

I roll a joint and I'm all psyched to smoke it with this guy Matt and his friend who is in town for the weekend from Chicago. Matt tells me his friend is named Lawyer and I'm thinking that's a stupid name and it'd be really stupid if he was in fact a lawyer but I don't ask him this, I pass him the joint and he smokes it between his cupped hands and I'm like oh, please. He says something about it being the proper way to smoke a joint because it's less harsh and you get a killer hit. Anyway, we get halfway through the joint and I'm getting ready to go into my pitch about this kind green bud that I have, this KGB, and how I'll cut them a good deal and all but that guy named Lawyer who is in town from Chicago for the weekend digs into his bulging sock and pulls out a bag of weed and says something about my stuff being amateur compared to this. And his weed smells up the entire room like a skunk in heat and it's green and he's like look at the crystals, and he starts to rubbing his fingers together and says something about THC and he's got this orange peel inside his bag and he mumbles something about the moisture, and it all just gives me a headache and I hate it when stuff like this happens. The scarf that Lawyer keeps draped around his neck even though he's inside and everything, that candy-stripped scarf starts to annoy the crap out of me and the more he talks the more I'm thinking I really don't like his stupid scarf and he goes on and on about how his bud should be smoked in a water pipe and he's like do you have a water pipe? And I'm thinking I'd like for him to leave now because that man Willie's deal is turning out to be not so sweet and my dad calls again and I look at the phone and I don't answer it. And that dude Lawyer stops going on about his crystal weed and the water pipe and he looks at the phone and he tells no one in particular that he hardly ever answers his phone.

I abruptly tell the two of them that I have to go out and I say it quick and brisk and I start to put on my coat and fidget with my keys and they're all high and aren't quite getting that they need to leave too, that they need to gather their crap and make like the wind. Matt looks at me and is like, when are you coming back? And so I tell him I have to head into the city and take care of some things. I tell him this and I look toward the window.

They reluctantly get up and we all leave together and then when we get to the train I tell them I forgot my wallet at home and I head back home to get my wallet that's sitting in my pocket. When I get home the phone rings and I just look at it. The caller ID tells me it's my dad and I just stare at the phone until it stops ringing.

CAFÉ NOIR

I'M TRYING TO FIGURE OUT WHAT THE HECK I'M DOING WRONG WITH MY LIFE BECAUSE THINGS AREN'T REALLY WORKING OUT and it was fine for a while but now it doesn't seem so fine and this glass of scotch is just about done and I want another one but I have like six dollars in my pocket and I need to tip this lady behind the bar who has been pouring my drinks. She's rather hot and it'd be a shame to not tip her but that cocktail would really help me figure out what the heck I need to do to get my life on track.

I'm nursing the rest of this booze and this type of thing sucks because I never have money and it's always enough money to get a taste but never enough to partake properly.

So, this one lady who is tending bar has a light-brownish reddish afro, her skin is honey brown, and she's just cute as pie and looks at me every so often and smiles. I'm in love with her. She asks me if I want another drink, and of course I want another scotch, but I tell her I'm okay and give a look as if to suggest that I'm done and how absurd it would be to have another cocktail, and so she clears away my glass that had one little bitty sip left and it's like the best part of the drink because it's got the right amount of scotch to the melted ice cubes and it's nice and cold and I can't fuss with her because she's fine and it'd seem pretty stupid because I just told her I'm okay and acted like I didn't want anything else to drink. I'm ridiculous and this proves it, and one day I'm going to write about this and everyone else will know how ridiculous I am.

Anyway, that lady with the honey-brown skin brings me another glass of scotch and says it's on her, and I don't say anything and try to look as if I'm contemplating drinking the drink but as soon as she moves away I drink the scotch.

She comes back over and tells me her name is Rosa and that seems like it'd be her name. Boy is she fine. She has no idea what a chump I am and I'm determined to not let her find out. I want her to think I hang at a place like this all the time and spend a hundred-fifty bucks on cocktails like it's no big thing, like all these other folks do who look to be from Spain or Italy or something and are all perfectly unshaven and wearing light-flowing clothing and are used to being out late and drinking champagne with gorgeous women until three in the morning on a Tuesday night and carrying on like they are.

I hang around because I'm really liking this Rosa lady and she keeps refilling my glass and I expect someone to tell me it's time to go because people are leaving and kissing each other on both cheeks and hugging, and Rosa kisses this guy and she introduces me to Flavio or something and he kisses me on both cheeks and winks to Rosa and says something to her in Spanish that I don't understand.

Anyway, the bouncer dude who has a whole mess of dreadlocks finally comes over and tells me to finish up, they're closing, but that honey-skin lady, the lady who said her name was Rosa, tells him I'm ok and the guy with the mess of dreds looks at me like he wants to say, not to me he's not.

I'm not really sure what being ok means but I act like I'm used to some sweetie telling some bouncer dude at four in the morning that I'm ok. So I stay on my stool and I drink my scotch. The bouncer dude pulls down the metal doors over the front windows and door and then someone behind me yells really loud and someone hands me a shot of some clear fluid and I drink it because that's what you're supposed to do. The clear fluid tastes like rocket fuel and is thick like syrup and I burp and it tastes the same, like thick licorice syrup.

Rosa asks me if I want to go have a cigarette and I tell her I do even though I don't smoke those things. I try and act like I do and I smoke one of them with Rosa who is just pure joy. She tells me she is glad she's off tomorrow and I tell her that's cool. She tells me she's looking forward to sleeping in and I tell her yeah, that'd be cool. I wish I could find something else to say but I can't. She asks me where I'm from and I tell her Brooklyn. She asks it again, like I'm supposed to be from Martinique or something, and I tell her Brooklyn even though I know she wants to know why my skin is browner than a white boy. She tells me she's from Cuba. And that seems about right. She looks like she is from Cuba and I'm thinking that Cuba would be a nice place to visit. Rosa tells me I should go to Cuba and I tell her that'd be cool and I feel stupid because that's all I seem to be able to say. She doesn't seem to mind and she grabs my hand and pulls me back inside this bar.

After a bunch more of those clear syrup shots I feel like I could vomit and I'm spinning around and I have to keep blinking my eyes to get them to stop this spinning thing.

Then the hiccups start and that's never a good thing. I go into the bathroom that has a stick of incense burning and the smell makes me feel nauseous. I do all the stuff you're supposed to do like splash water on your face and I try to open my eye holes as wide as possible but everything is moving, the sink, the toilet, my face, my hands and gravity is just playing with my mind and I have a feeling it's going to be one of those nights.

Rosa asks me to walk her home and she's got this bicycle that's all old school from the 80's with a basket on the front and she changes her mind after a couple blocks, so I throw it in the back of a taxi and she tells me to get in so I do. The taxi driver seems to be swerving to hit potholes like it's some type of video game that gives bonus points for slamming into ditches in the road. Rosa is talking and going on about something and I can't follow a word she is saying because my head is leaned towards the open window and the wind is crashing into my ears.

We get to her place somewhere in the East Village and I help hoist the bike out of the trunk and she pays the driver and sends him off. A very good thing but not a great thing because I'm certain I'm going to vomit and that can really crush any hopes of me and Rosa. We go into her apartment and I feel as though I'm on some kind of merry-go-round and that's about how my life feels. Like a merry-go-round.

I go into Rosa's bathroom and I look at my penis and it's all shrunken up and blue like it's not well and I look into the mirror and my face looks about the same. I hiccup and it hurts, and everything is moving, so I close my eyes and brace myself on the sink. I can hear that Rosa has put on some music and it's like salsa or something, and all percussive, and when I get in the other room she's dancing around like she doesn't have a care in the world, and the music keeps saying something like baila contigo, and I'm praying she doesn't think I'm going to baila contigo. She lights a cigarette for me and I puff it and I realize my lips are numb. I hiccup and I accidentally inhale the smoke from the cigarette which makes me gag so I go into the bathroom again and run water because I'm thinking about booting into the toilet but it's all cramped into the corner and I start to thinking about all I ate that night, the olives, the lamb kabobs, that white yogurt sauce, the hummus, the cheese, the peanuts, and it all comes back to the licorice syrup which I taste every time I hiccup.

I come back into the room and Rosa has changed into one of those long shirts and I can see her nipples through it as if they are taunting me because I'm never going to be able to see this thing through.

Next thing I know I'm on her futon on the floor of her bedroom and I wish I could tell you there was passion. I wish I could tell you I hit it and all that, but I was spinning like a draidl. Rosa turned off the lights and pulled me on top of her and I kissed her neck a bit and hiccuped and then she kind of got the picture and fell off asleep. I got up because I hiccuped and got a mouthful of vomit and dashed for the front door and down the steps. When I got like half a block away I tossed my bowels all over the street, all over the sidewalk, and then I looked down and I had splattered vomit all over my socks and realized I left my shoes behind. I looked up at this door that had a blue light over it and it said something about the Hells Angels Headquarters so I moved briskly away and crossed the street and was nearly slammed by a taxi that skidded out ten feet from me.

A dude came out of that place that said Hells Angels and he cursed over his shoulder and two dudes with big bellies and big beards came out, looked at the sidewalk and then came running across the street after me. I ran as fast as possible towards Second Avenue and turned another corner and hid in between two cars. I was trying to keep as quiet as possible but every so often I'd hiccup.

After a while I peeked up and through the windshield and saw a big dude looking up and down the block. I ducked down and was certain he saw me and was certain I was going to get pulled into some basement, and images of Pulp Fiction shot through my mind. I kept low and moved further up the block and broke out in a full sprint to the next block and ran half the way home in my tube socks.

I stopped before crossing the Brooklyn Bridge and realized my hiccups were gone. My heart pounded away. It seemed as if, at least for now, things were ok.

THE P.A.

THERE'S A MAN IN FRONT OF ME AND I'M NOT SURE IF HE'S KIDDING OR IF THIS IS SOME KIND OF INSIDE JOKE OR SOME WEIRD TEST OR SOMETHING, SO I DON'T KNOW WHETHER OR NOT I SHOULD SMILE. I'm trying to gauge the reactions of the people surrounding him. There's this one lady whose arms poke out from a white fleece vest who is always hollering into these stupid radios, which they make all of us carry, and there's this special lingo where you have to say *copy this* and *copy that* and it's a whole thing and some people just get carried away with this stuff like we're in the military or something and it's always annoying. Anyway, this man that is in front of me has asked that I get him a piece of dairy-free flourless angel food cake and I'm not sure what I'm supposed to say because all day I've been doing things and getting stuff for people and it's a pain in the ass this film production thing that I'm working on. That lady with the fleece vest barked my name into the radio that's plugged into my ear and there's like ten or twelve other people who are like me and they call us P.A.'s and that stands for production assistant and it basically means we do everything that other people don't want to do, like get coffee and drive these fifteen passenger vans and get ice and take lunch orders and carry crap for people who don't want to carry stuff, and we are the first ones on set and the last ones to leave at like four in the morning.

I thought this would be a pretty cool job because it's this commercial for some kitchen product and we're in this mansion on Central Park East and my friends seemed to think it was pretty cool to be doing something like this and so I thought it's pretty cool, but now this man who everyone tells me is the director and executive producer is asking me to do something and I'm thinking, why are they picking on me? I now realize they like me because I do everything they tell me to do and the other people who are P.A.'s like myself hang out by this truck and smoke cigarettes and drink all kinds of coffee and talk about other jobs they've been on and tell each other how many hours the music video was and about the crane that hung off the side of the building and whatnot, and after two days of this nonsense it's making me think that this job is not pretty cool.

One of the things that I'm finding confusing is that each time they shoot something there's this protocol and they fuss with this and that and then fuss some more with the wardrobe of the "talent," which in this case is a woman who is holding a baby and she's talking about whatever she's talking about and they're trying to make decisions as to what shirt she should be wearing and what color belt, and things that seem just innocuous, and it's what all these fine folks get paid to do and they go back and forth with the shirt until the guy who is fussing with the camera informs them that they'll never see the belt in frame and then they mumble about it some more until this guy yells into his radio, *lock it up* and that means stand still and stop talking and then they say, *roll sound* and a guy with headphones says, *sound rolls* and then that guy says, *roll camera* and the hippy dude with a pony tail holding the camera says, *camera has speed* and then that director says *action* and the guy standing next to him says *action* and then the lady drops the box of cleaner and then picks it up and they say *keep rolling,* and after she does what she's supposed to do they say *cut* and the director dude says *beautiful, excellent, perfect* and then says *let's go again right away* and it's starting to bother me that he says everything is excellent and beautiful and perfect and then wants to do it again because it seems to me if it's perfect and excellent we should be done already but that's not what happens and he keeps saying *let's try it one more time* and then the next time he says *let's try it one more time* and it's starting to drive me nuts because I want to go home and take a dump.

Anyway, the executive producer, director man whose ass everyone is kissing and who seems to like this dynamic, wears those glasses with the clear frames and has on a denim buttoned-down shirt that says something about Sundance Film Festival on it and he's somewhere in his forties and probably skis in Aspen and wears those ridiculous big furry boots and thinks it's cool. So, this guy, he says to me that he'd like a dairy-free, flourless piece of angel food cake and I'm trying to figure out if he is serious or if this is some kind of inside joke thing or a set-up, and when I say that I will get the cake, money will exchange hands and it's some gag and they'll all fall out laughing and they'll say I told you so and talk about the last guy who they asked to get dairy free, flourless angel food cake and said no and I'm looking at these folks for some sign that this could be the case and show them I'm not falling for it but they just stand around and continue to kiss his butt like it's a goddamn scoop of ice cream, but the folks who are kissing his butt and standing around him just look at me and I'm thinking that the guy with the clear glasses is serious and I say to him, dairy-free cake? And the guy with the clear glasses purses his lips and says, diary-free, flourless angel food cake, make it happen, and he says it all quick and then he goes to his cell and starts texting someone, somewhere.

I swallow and turn around because that's what you do when you're a P.A. and some director dude with clear glasses tells you to get something that probably doesn't exist and if it does why would you want it anyways? I mean, give me a fucking break, y'know, why would you want a piece of cake that is all good for you? I ask the lady with the fleece vest where I should get this piece of cake and she says she has no idea and she's confident that I should be able to find it and I'm thinking that maybe I shouldn't have been running about like I did, being all good at what I'm doing because now I've got to get the guy with the clear glasses a piece of stupid cake because I was the guy working hard. And this is what happens when you do what you're supposed to do.

So I walk by the truck with the other P.A.'s and they are carrying on about the other shoot they were on with Sarah Jessica Parker and I'm like give me a break. I Google flourless angel food cake New York City and it's nothing but nonsense that comes up. Something about a dairy-free store in lower Manhattan and then some bakery that specializes in this business of special order pastries that are gluten-free and whatnot but it's way early in the morning and I'm way tired and I'm contemplating going home and smoking a joint and playing PlayStation.

After about two hours, at nine a.m., I find the stupid cake. And the place I get it from looks like the type of place this director guy would go to on like a Sunday morning or something and it just bothers me, but I get the cake and I hustle back to that mansion because the lady with the fleece vest has called me like nine times.

I get back to set and I'm thinking that I'm like super P.A. and I got this dude the flourless cake and it's in this nice little bag and the guy at the place wrapped it all nice like it was some kind of gift, but when I get back to set everyone is on lunch and my grand entrance with the cake is not so grand. That lady with the fleece vest asks me what took so long and I don't really know what to say to that so I tell her something about traffic. Then she tells me she called me a ton of times and I stand there and do that thing with my face, the thing that says I have no idea what you're talking about and then she tells me to set the cake on this little area near these monitors where the director sits and then she tells me to fill up a cooler with ice and then mop up the bathroom because there's a leak under the toilet.

The dude with the clear glasses doesn't speak to me or thank me or anything. He continues with the excellent, let's do it again thing, and I go over there at some point and the flourless cake is in the garbage, uneaten, and it just seems to me that there are better things I could be doing with my time.

SI, THE VIDEO GUY

IT'S NOT AS IF I DON'T KNOW WHAT THE RED LIGHT MEANS. I understand what REC is, it means the camera is recording. I get it. I mean, it's not as if I haven't used this camera a bunch of times. Okay, it is my first wedding, sure, I'm not saying I've shot weddings before but I've used this camera to shoot other stuff like my brother's graduation, and my band and so forth. Thing is, you push the red button on the side of the camera and the stupid thing is rolling. I pushed the button at the end of the ceremony and the red REC light came on and this leads me to believe that the camera hasn't been rolling, and this is a problem. That's where the problem is.

I'm thinking about the guy Si—short for Simon—who sent me out on this job, who is going to send me out on a whole bunch of jobs this summer. He was looking for a videographer, and I responded to his advertisement. I called him and he asked that I come over to his place. So I did. His operation was in his house out in Jersey. Upstairs around back. Si is a tank of a guy and doesn't look the type to be making sentimental wedding videos but that's what he does, it's how he makes a living, and from the size of his house and the amount of digital video equipment it looks as if he's got a good thing going. Si, the Video Guy. That's what it says on his business card.

Si asks me stuff about my experience and I lie because I need this job. I tell him I've shot a bunch of weddings and parties and stuff. I tell him I've got a whole lot of experience and I show him this tape of a friend's wedding and I tell him that I was the one who shot it, even though I wasn't.

I get the job. Si is impressed by the tape and asks if he could hold onto it, which I'm not too excited about, but I am excited when he opens up a calendar and starts asking me about my availability. He asks me if I have the following weekend open and I tell him yes, and I open my calendar and pretend that I have some kind of schedule when I don't.

Si prints out a list of things I need to do. He tells me to arrive an hour early at the church and to get some exterior shots. He shows me a tape of a wedding and shows me what an exterior shot is and I see that it is an outside shot of the church, and he tells me to tilt down off the sky to the church all pretty-like and then zoom into the door on the outside of the church, and that this is the first shot that I'll shoot. He tells me I need to take this small box with a wire on it and a tiny microphone at the end and attach the microphone to the groom. He shows me how I should do this. There's an antenna on the little microphone box and he says that it's wireless, and there is this other box that is a bit larger and he tells me this is the receiver, and I act as if I know this even though I don't. Then Si asks that I should mic him up and he stands up and stares at me until I get up and take the little mic and try to fasten it to his shirt and he's all breathing in my face while I'm trying to do this and his chest is all hairy and his breath smells like a tobacco pipe and dark coffee. My hands are moving and shaking even though I don't want them to and then Si snatches the mic from me and tells me I'm doing it wrong and then he looks at me all hard like he's trying to figure out if I'm full of shit so I look back at him as best I can to hide the fact that yes, I am full of shit. After a little of this Si fastens the mic to my shirt like you're supposed to do it and I mumble something about the mics I normally use are different.

Si tells me I need to wear a tuxedo. He says I should wear a tuxedo and black shoes, no black sneakers. My dad gave me this tuxedo and I never thought I'd wear it because it's too small and the pants barely hit my ankles and the sleeves barely make it to my wrists, but today I'm in this costume. I look ridiculous in this tuxedo my dad gave me, but it's what I'm supposed to wear so I wear it.

So I do what he tells me. I find this church up in the Bronx, after getting lost and motoring around the Bronx on a road called the Major Deegan Expressway for close to an hour. I get to this church and I shoot that exterior shot and it's pretty simple this job. No one leaning over my shoulder. No one hollering at me in some radio or something. I just shoot an exterior shot of this big church.

I find the groom and I put that microphone on him and I do this shot that Si told me to get where the groom and his groomsmen shake hands and stuff, and I shoot that and then I do an arrival of the bride when she gets there in this oversized white limousine. Her dad is with her and he's this big Greek man with hairy arms, and tufts of hair coming up out the back of his shirt. He glares at me and I get the sense that he's forking over a whole lot of money for me to be there and he doesn't seem too happy about this so I look like you should look when someone is forking over a whole lot of money - I try to look all professional, and he looks at me like he'd like to ring my neck.

Anyway, the ceremony begins and people are crying and the priest looks regal and the bride is frantic and the groom is sweaty, and they go through this whole thing and the priest is talking in Greek and English and flicks water on the couple, and the groom has to wear this crown and walk about, and I'm shooting all of this from the back of the church, and then he says something in Greek and the two of them kiss and everyone is all happy and crying and whatnot, and then it's pretty clear this part of the day is over, and I press the red button on the camera to end the recording and that red REC light comes on and I'm terrified that I wasn't rolling, and my heart does that flutter thing and I'm thinking about that man Si and the tattoos on his arms that are all weathered looking and the ink that is faded, and they say something about the Marine Corps and Korea. I don't like these thoughts. I don't like the idea of upsetting Si. Guys like Si aren't even keeled and aren't reasonable and I've gotten myself into a situation where I'll most likely see how angry that man Si can get. I have a burning feeling Si is going to be in a rage and I would really like to just go away. And I wish I had never answered that advertisement. I wish I never knew a man named Si who does wedding videos. But I do. Here we go again.

I have directions to this reception hall somewhere farther out in the Bronx and I get in my car and drive away. I stop at a little bar called Blarney Stone and go inside with the camera bag on my shoulder. The bartender sets a glass of beer in front of me and I take the camera out and press the button that says rewind and it doesn't rewind for more than a few seconds and that's not good news. Turns out I wasn't rolling on the ceremony. Nothing that I thought I shot exists on tape. This is bad. It is the kind of news that you order a shot and a beer over. Turns out I did roll on the exterior shot and that's just not going to cut it, and I'm thinking that I shouldn't have smoked that joint on my way to the Bronx.

I have to decide what to do. I need to come up with an excuse. I have to figure a way out of this situation.

So, I go to the reception hall and people are all festive and it's cocktail hour and that's what people are doing - they are drinking cocktails - and I'm shooting them doing this and I have to get shots of the food like Si told me to get. I get shots of the food before people eat it, and he showed me how he likes it to look when he showed me that tape, and I do it like he likes. I shoot the melon and prosciutto, and the scallops wrapped in bacon, and the fried shrimps, and the clams casino and whatnot. I make sure that red light that says REC is on, and it is. The tape is rolling. But I have that sinking feeling. I feel like shit.

I feel bad because it's like their special day and I messed it up because I didn't hit the record button. Years from now when they are gathered on their twenty-fifth wedding anniversary they will remember me, the guy who didn't hit record, and all they'll have is the exterior shot of the church that zooms into the door, and shots of prosciutto and melon, and their children will ask where's the ceremony and they will remember me. Years from now they will remember the guy who didn't record the wedding and that's just the way it's going to be because the ceremony happened and it's not going to happen again. That's it.

Salvatore the DJ is there and he asks me how the ceremony went and I tell him it was nice. I tell him it was at this Greek church in the Bronx and Sal tells me that he'll catch my eye before he plays *YMCA* and the *Electric Slide* and he tells me he will make sure I'm in position when it's time to cut the cake and do the bouquet. Sal is OK. He knows Si pretty good. He knows Si likes to have shots of people carrying on to the *Electric Slide* and to *YMCA*.

It's a long drive home at the end of a long night of the *Macarena,* and drunk relatives saying stuff into camera about having a nice life together and being happy and remembering to always love one another and I'm thinking that I'll probably never have that, I'll probably never have a wedding and if I do I won't have drunk relatives saying stuff to a camera guy.

I drop the tapes off at Si's. I know it's the first and last time I will do that. This is the end of this job. So I drop the tapes and I haul ass out of there. I get out as quickly as possible before his dog starts to hollering and all. I get out of there.

When Si calls on Tuesday and says that there must be a tape missing I play along. I tell him I'll look in my car. He is irate and he tells me he needs that tape. I can't tell him what happened. These phone calls go on for like two weeks until I tell him I don't know where the tape is. I dropped it on his back porch. All the tapes, I tell him. I tell him there's nowhere it could possibly be.

I never call Si about picking up my money from that job. I hope he didn't charge that Greek man. Si never calls me back even though I had jobs on the calendar.

THE GNOME

I NEED MY RENT MONEY BEFORE THE FIFTEENTH, THIS MAN SAYS TO ME. He's my landlord and he lives beneath me in the basement apartment with his wife and dogs. I don't know how many dogs and I don't know what they look like because I've never seen them but I've heard them. I've heard them at three, four, five o'clock in the morning. Howling and moaning. It sounds as if they are conjuring demons. I've told my landlord about the dogs that howl and moan in the middle of the night and my landlord wiggles the toothpick that's plugged into the side of his mouth and looks at me like he doesn't know what I'm talking about, and I look at him like how could you not know what I'm talking about when I hear the dogs howling upstairs in my flat, and you live in the same room as them, I guess, unless he and his wife are not home at three, four, five o'clock in the morning. There is no way they could not hear the dogs howling. And I can't think of a reason why they wouldn't be home at that ungodly hour. What could possibly be going on down there?

I've seen my landlord in his ugly light-blue van out on the street. It's a beat-up old Dodge with a mangled wire coat hanger antenna. I've seen it idling near our apartment and I've looked in the window and seen my landlord in there, just sitting there staring straight ahead as if he's forgotten that he's sitting in a van idling. My landlord's name is Owen Cabot. He looks like a gnome and is squat and has one of them thick mountain man beards and a thick bowl cut brown head of hair like he's out of some Hobbit movie or something. I can't complain to the Hobbit about the dogs right now because my rent is months overdue. He tells me I'm months behind and then he tells me he needs his rent money by the fifteenth, and now I have to avoid him and check up and down the block when I enter and exit my apartment building because I don't want to run into him. My brother paid his portion of the rent but he's not trying to put up for me and I don't blame him. My brother put up for me before and this is the way it is, I don't have money. I gotta find a job.

Two years ago when my landlord showed us the apartment there were these disturbing paintings in the common stairwell. And when I say disturbing I mean awful garish colors and portions of faces all distorted and snarled looking, and thick oil paint that looks slapped on too thick. They look like some demonic nightmare from hell. I purposely look to the ground when I enter and exit my apartment because they aren't what you want to see when you're starting or ending your day. They are the landlord's wife's paintings. I'm shocked that she considers herself a painter. I'm shocked that she has the audacity to put these framed images in the hallway of their apartment building. The only use I can see, and this isn't much of a stretch, is that if a thief was breaking into this building and looked up and saw these fucked-up paintings, he might turn around and leave. My brother has threatened more than a handful of times to take them down. That lady who is married to our landlord runs a florist business and does big high-end corporate jobs and I just don't get it. My brother says he's seen her walking the streets drunk and mumbling to herself, and I'm like, where? And he tells me up and down Seventh Avenue and I'm like, shut up, and he shrugs his shoulders as if to show me that he doesn't care if I believe him or not, and so I say, get out of here, and he just flips channels on the television, and then I ask him why, because I want to keep the conversation afloat and figure out who the hell lives below my room, and he's like, why what? And I can't seem to make sense of these two folks and their demon dogs that howl through the night.

I come home and my landlord's wife is parked on the steps in the common stairwell and she smells like vodka and not like a couple of drinks of vodka, she smells like she's been bingeing for a couple few days, because it's coming out her pours and her lips look all glossy and wet and swollen and red like folks who drink vodka for days look. I know she's there because she needs to collect my rent money and now is drunked up and who knows what kind of trouble she's going to start. I'm thinking she must want some cash to get another bottle of vodka. I'm cold busted because she's been there waiting for me to come home and I don't have the money because I can't find a job. I'm trying to think of the best way to tell her this when she tells me she lost her key and can't get into her apartment. I'm relieved, but then I'm thinking that I hope she doesn't think she's staying in my place. I'm feeling all put on the spot because it's cold out and she's looking all pathetic like she's homeless and I'm like, do you want to use the phone? I'm trying to sound all accommodating and hospitable because I owe them a whole gang of money and she's like, I want to get into my apartment, and she tells me she can get into her place through the back door in our kitchen and I'm like, oh? Then I remember the door in the kitchen, and I remember that it doesn't have a lock on it, so my brother had shoved a bunch of crap up against the door so no one could get up into our place. So, I move all the crap and that lady stumbles down into her apartment and I'm like, see you later, and I catch a glimpse of their apartment that looks all dark and musty. I shut the door and put all the crap back up against the door and I'm wondering why these folks live down in the basement when they own an entire brownstone and I'm thinking what kind of a place is it down there because it sounds as if they have three or four dogs and then the two of them, and the place can't be all that big.

I have to find a job and this one lady named Anika tells me to go to a temp agency because they'll pay you that week, which is exactly what I need, so I have got to get to that temp agency. I don't have money for the train. This is how broke I am. I'm so broke I don't even have money to get on the goddamn train to go and try to get a job from this temp agency. I go up into my brother's room, and shovel change off his dresser into my hand. I see some silver and some quarters so I'm thinking I'm in pretty good shape. I ride the F train to 42nd Street and get up out the train and look for 450 Madison Avenue, which is actually on 42nd Street, not Madison Avenue. I go up into this outfit called Quality Temps. I go in the door and there are all kinds of folks sitting in chairs looking as pathetic as myself. The guys have leather jackets over shirts and ties, print sweaters with button-down shirts poking out of the collars, worn-looking black shoes, and worn-looking brown shoes, while the ladies are in dresses, solid muted colors, with half-ass looking hems that are bunched up just over the knees and platform shoes that look torturous on their stocking covered feet. I'm a bit disturbed by the age range of these folks who are out of work. Some of them look to be around my age but then there are folks that look middle-aged but in their forties, and it's just sad, and then there are folks who look to be in their fifties and sixties and that just bothers me, and what if I'm like fifty and out of work and I have to go to some sad-ass place called Quality Temps to try and find a job? But that's never going to happen because I'm in a band and once we get our record deal I'll be set up for life.

I go to what I think is the front desk and there is a lady behind the desk who talks on the phone and doesn't look at me. She says to whoever she's on the phone with, no you di-in't, and then she says it again an octave higher, and then the lady behind the desk says, nu-uh, a couple of times, smacks her gum three times quick, and then swivels her chair and flips one leg up over the other leg and pushes a clipboard in my direction without looking at me. This lady has nails that stick two to three inches off the end of her fingers and are a mixture of three gaudy unmentionable colors, and there's sparkly stuff and a little fake heart diamond stud in the middle of her thumbnail. Her hair is slapped across the front of her forehead in either direction and pushed toward the ears, and then falls not quite to her shoulders and I bet she pays someone good money for this hairstyle. I bet she gets her hair did once a week to look like this. I bet she coughs up a whole gang of cash to have this done to her hair.

There is a sheet of paper on the clipboard that looks as if it'd been photocopied eight hundred times and I strain my eyes to make sense of it. It has all the usual stuff about name, address, phone number, recent employment and whatnot—all the stuff that is on my resume—so after a while I begin filling in the blank spaces with the words, "see resume." I hand the lot of it back to the lady with the nails who ignored my presence, and she glances at the paper, flips it over and frowns. Then she does the unthinkable and speaks to me. She tells me I need to fill out each section, and I try to tell her that the same information in those sections is on my resume, but she has already gone back to her phone conversation and swivels her chair away from me. I do what she tells me to do because that's what you do when you're unemployed, you do what you're told to do and you do it with a smile on your face.

II

I'm trying to get a hold of my brother and I can't, and this is a terribly messed up situation I'm in and I really need to speak to him. I really need him to bail me out, but he's not answering his phone and I can't figure out why. Where could he possibly be? How could he possibly not answer his phone? If I can't get in touch with him, I'm screwed.

I'm in a wrinkled, blue dress shirt that I found in the back of my brother's closet, and grey tie, and I'm wearing a V-neck undershirt beneath this shirt, and I have pleated khakis on that are bloused, and church socks that make my feet sweat inside these stupid, uncomfortable shoes. I'm in this room by myself and there are no windows.

I get a call from that temp agency and they send me to this address and tell me to see some lady named Lucy LaTerra, so I go there and tell that to the receptionist, and this lady comes out from the glass doors and she's all pleasant and chipper and everything and says her name is Lucy LaTerra, and she tells me to follow her, so I do what she asks. Her hair is what they call frosted and the roots are black like she couldn't care less, and I couldn't care less because I really, desperately need cash from this job because it pays $15 an hour, and with that bit of change I'll be able to pay my rent and then I can complain to my landlord about his dogs that keep me up in the middle of the night howling and whatnot.

Anyway, I follow this lady with the black roots back through the glass doors and she walks really fast and she's balancing a coffee that has a big pink lipstick print on the plastic lid and I'm trying to walk with her but then I let her get a few steps in front of me, which seems to work out okay because she talks loudly and I can still hear her. I'm extra polite and amiable because I need to work and I'm desperate and that's the way you act when you're out of work. This lady tells me she has this job that lasts three days and this is the first day. I act all interested when really I could give a fuck. She points out the kitchen area where she tells me there are beverages and snacks and coffee and tells me to help myself to anything I want, and then we turn up a hall and make a right up another hall, and everything looks the same and there are tons of these little cubicles with carpet on the walls and there are a bunch of empty desks with empty chairs, and I'm trying to remember which way we came so I can get back to that kitchen with the snacks, and then she opens a door, flicks on the fluorescent lights and tells me this is where I'll be sitting. There's hardly anyone else in the entire office and I'm wondering what kind of operation they're running but I'm not going to ask her because it's none of my business.

Lucy LaTerra asks me if I'm proficient in wizzy-something or other and I'm like, excuse me? And she says they told me you're familiar with wizzy-wig, and she's starting up the computer that's on the desk and she's arranging the keyboard and whatnot and I'm like yeah, definitely, and she seems pleased with this, so I'm thinking it must be some kind of computer thing. I discover that it is some kind of computer thing and it's something that I'm not familiar with and now I can't go back to Lucy LaTerra and tell her I haven't a clue what wizzy-wig is because I already told her that I am familiar with it and I've been sitting at this desk for close to three hours and that's $45, and I can't go up to her now after all this time has expired because she'll be like, what the heck have you been doing all this time? I should've told her I didn't know what wizzy-wig is right off the bat and maybe I would've gotten the job anyway and maybe I wouldn't, but at least I wouldn't be sweating it out in some office feeling like I feel.

So I sit in the office and look busy when Lucy LaTerra passes by and she's passed by a number of times and smiled and is very pleasant and she asks me how things are going and I try to look all busy and I tell her everything is fine even though it's not fine because I'm in some program called WYSIWYG and it makes no sense and there's a stack of papers and I have no idea what the heck I'm supposed to be doing with all these papers but I shuffle them around and make three different piles and when that lady pokes her head in the door and looks at the different piles she seems pleased so I keep arranging papers every so often, and I call my brother every five minutes because he is the only person who can make sense of this stupid computer thing but he's not answering his phone.

Lucy LaTerra tells me I should take a lunch and I'm like, I'm okay, and I make a face to suggest that eating is a silly idea because I am here to work and I go through all this rigamarole because I don't want to leave my desk because if she comes into the room while I'm gone and looks at my computer screen, I'm fucked. She tells me she's going downstairs to get lunch and asks me if she can pick anything up for me and I'm starved to hell and back but I have about $2.30 in nickels and dimes, and first of all, it's embarrassing to give someone all that change to pick you up some chips or whatever, and second of all, I need that money to get back home on the train. Lucy LaTerra tells me that I should eat, and I'd love to tell her she's right, and then she asks me what I want, and says you have to eat, and I wave her off and tell her I'm fine because I don't know what will happen if I ask her to pick me up a corned beef sandwich on rye with mustard and a pickle, which is what I want more than I've wanted anything in my entire life, but she might be like, that's $8.50, so I lie and tell her I'm fine and I do my best to look as though I'm fine. I do my best to look as if eating is absurd, even though my stomach is growling like a hog in heat.

I wait a couple of minutes and then I venture out to find the kitchen with the snacks. There are a few people in the cubicles now and they seem to be working on their computers or whatever. One man takes a look at me and it is pretty apparent that I'm lost so he asks if he can help me, and I tell him I'm looking for the kitchen. He tells me to take a left and then the second right, so I do what he tells me and I find the kitchen and I don't see any snacks. There's a candy machine with a base price of 75 cents and that is out of my league. Someone was kind enough to leave some saltine crackers in a drawer that must've been left over from their soup or something. I shove those in the pocket of my pleated pants, then I rifle through another drawer and come up empty - just condiments, sugar, powdered creamer for coffee and such. I crank open the refrigerator door and rummage around. I catch a foul whiff of some bad food, and my eyes rake across a Chinese takeout container that has a dark grease stain on the bottom and a wilted bean sprout hanging from an opening in the top. There is a sign on the door that declares that food left past Friday at 4 p.m. will be trash. I find a brown paper bag with the name Roger scrawled across the front on a piece of masking tape, an old banana, a couple of yogurts, and a piece of lemon. There is half a sandwich inside Roger's bag and I'm thinking I could slide out a piece of the meat and slap in on my crackers. I open the sandwich and the meat smells gamey so I shove it back inside. The slap-slap of heels startles me and I spin around, cold busted. It is Lucy LaTerra and she has a bag of food in one hand and a fresh coffee in the other. She asks me if I want part of her sandwich, and she tells me she'll never finish it. I have to tell her no because I already told her I'm not hungry. I already went through this whole thing about how I'm not hungry and now I have to stick with it. I tell her I was looking for a soda and she tells me there is a soda machine right there and she points to the machine next to the snack machine. I look at the oversized machine as if seeing it for the first time and then I rummage through my change and start counting out nickels and dimes and I'm hoping she leaves so I don't actually have to buy a soda because that will leave me with no money to get the train home, but she doesn't leave, she fusses with her sandwich and tosses out the overabundance of meat, which just kills me. She carries on about this and that, and now another lady is in the kitchen and she's carrying on as well, and I'm still rummaging through my change, killing time, praying she leaves so I don't have to purchase the soda, and then Lucy introduces me to that other lady who says her name is Olivia and she's a big lady with big sweaty hands and I shake her sweaty hand that's the size of a catcher's mitt and now I have to buy the soda and get the hell out of there, so I do.

Anyway, this is the way my life is but it's okay because I'm the drummer in this kick-ass band and one day we are going to be huge and we'll have a video on MTV and this lady will be like, I remember him, that guy who is playing drums in the video, he was that guy who didn't eat and lied about knowing WYSIWYG.

I type stuff into the computer and save it and then I have no idea where the information is saved, but that doesn't matter anyway because I'm not sure what I'm supposed to be doing but it makes me look busy and I'm just biding my time until my brother answers his goddamn phone. I try rebooting the computer, I try to find a help menu, I call my brother, I unplug the computer and then plug it back in, and then I call my brother, I scroll down and enter information into a box and then I call my brother. Lucy LaTerra comes back into the room and says that I can save my material to this disk that she hands me. I try to smile back at her and then tilt the computer screen away from her like it's no big deal. She leaves and I call my brother and he answers the phone and he's like, what? And I'm all panicked and trying to sound calm and I ask him if he knows what WYSIWYG is and he says it's a computer program and I'm like yes it is a computer program, and then I ask him if he is familiar with it and he says, why? And I really want to reach through the phone and choke him but I have to remain calm and even-keeled and see if I can get my brother to play ball. I tell him that I'm on a temp job and I need to use WYSIWYG, and he tells me it is an application, and I want to scream because I don't care what it is, I just need to know how to use it very quickly because it is three o'clock in the afternoon and I have no idea what I'm doing and I'm starved and irritable because all I've had is some stupid crackers and a can of orange soda that I couldn't afford and now I have no train fare, so I either have to jump the subway turnstile and possibly get arrested or walk eight miles home to Brooklyn in the dead of winter. My brother tells me he doesn't understand how I got the job if I didn't know the application and then I tell him I didn't know that I needed to use the program and this lady was misinformed and thought I knew how to use it and I just went with it, and what difference does it make anyway, and he goes on and says, I don't get it, and I feel like telling him that there's nothing to get but I let him go on about how he doesn't understand and everything because if I get him pissed he won't help me. I ask him if he could talk me through the program so I can enter this information into the computer and he tells me that I'm a buffoon, and I don't respond. He tells me that he only has a minute because he is working on a programming assignment that is due in the morning and I am glad that he doesn't have much time so he can be quick about helping me out of my situation. He asks me what I see on the screen and I describe what I see, and I can hear that he doesn't really feel like doing this but it is somewhat entertaining to him that I should be at some office in midtown Manhattan and I don't know what the heck I'm doing. He asks me what I'm supposed to be doing anyway and I'm trying to tell him I have no idea, and he says he doesn't understand. Finally he talks me though the basic functions and menus and it's of no help and I'm starting to think that I should probably figure out some kind of exit strategy because it's almost four o'clock and the real problem is that I wasted six hours futzing with this program and now it's almost time to go home and I'm nowhere near where I should be with my assignment, and how do I explain this to Lucy LaTerra and still fill out a time card with a good conscience and get paid, and I'm thinking that isn't going to happen so I ball up my coat and head like I'm going to the bathroom and slip out the exit and go home.

It's a hell of a long walk from midtown Manhattan to Brooklyn. A hell of a long walk. Bad shoes. Bad. Bad shoes. I can no longer feel my feet. I could cry from the ache. My feet are numb.

When I get home my brother is like, what happened with that job, and I tell him nothing happened and he turns and goes back upstairs. My feet are cramped and sweaty and I am going to burn these shoes, but I'm too damn tired from walking eight miles on cold hard concrete.

I call after my brother and ask him why there is an orange power cord dangling over the railing from upstairs and going all the way back to my room and he tells me not to touch it and to just leave it alone. Don't touch it, he says again. He pokes his head downstairs and I ask him what will happen if I touch it and he just looks at me all serious and deadpan, and that's supposed to show me that he is for real.

My brother tells me he has to run some kind of deck and another computer upstairs for this assignment due in the morning and there's not enough power up in his room so he needs to tap into another circuit, which happens to be in my room, and then, as if on cue, the power dies out in the entire apartment. It's pretty dark outside so I can only see my brother's silhouette but I'm willing to bet good money his face is crimson. He stomps up into his room and I call after him and ask what happened because I want to hear just how frustrated he is and I want to laugh but it's not time for that just yet. I hear him up there fussing with plugs and everything and he is making a racket and I'm thinking he's pretty frustrated but the kicker will be if he lost everything he was working on and that'd suck because he's been working on whatever it is he's been working on all day. I see a flashlight beam poking through the darkness up there and I go to the refrigerator and it's dark in there too and I'm thinking about food going sour and then I remember there isn't much food in there anyways, just some condiments and a pitcher of water that needs its filter changed because there's black pebbly things all in the filter chamber and on the floor of the pitcher.

My brother stomps back downstairs and he's all salty and he's searching for the circuit breaker and he says something about patching into something else or whatever, and he's shining that stupid light in my face and I block the light with my hand and he searches the walls for clues as to where the circuit breaker is. He walks out into the hallway and when he opens the door a shaft of light spills into the apartment and I hear him go up the stairs and he's continuing up and up and then after a while he stomps back down. He tells me the lady who lives upstairs said she thinks the breaker is down in the basement so my brother goes out to the front of the building and rings the bell of the basement apartment where the squat landlord and his drunk wife live. Then he goes to their door and knocks, and then knocks again harder this time. No one answers, just the demon dogs howling and everything, and my brother comes back inside and flicks on that stupid flashlight and now he's rummaging around a drawer in the kitchen and he asks me if I have a number for that man downstairs and I tell him no. He finds their number after a while and dials the number into the phone and we can both hear the phone ringing downstairs and it just rings and rings and the stupid dogs are down there fussing around and howling.

My brother shines the light on me and tells me to go downstairs and flip on the breaker. I look at him because there's no way I'm going down there, and I contort my face to suggest this and my brother tells me to get down there, and there's no way I'm going down there so I just lay back on the couch and fold my arms behind my head so he knows that it's absolutely out of the question. I tell *him* to go down there and I ask him what's the big deal, just go down there I tell him, and he says, exactly, it's no big deal, go down there and hit the breaker, and he's trying to be all convincing but it's not really my problem because I don't have an assignment due in the morning and I can do without power for the time being. We go back and forth like this for a bit because that's what we do and it's pretty clear that I'm not going down there and it's pretty clear that nothing is going to happen unless he goes down there. I'm praying that he does because there's really nothing else happening because I can't watch television and I can't listen to music and it'd be really entertaining to me if my brother went down into the landlord's apartment and got bit by one of those mangy dogs or it'd be pretty funny if the landlord came home while he was down there fussing about and was like, what the hell are you doing in my place? I encourage him to get down there so I ask him things like, what time is the assignment due? And I ask him where he thinks the landlord is and stuff like that. Then he goes over to where the door leading downstairs is and he starts to fussing with the crap in front of the door and I'm like, good, and this gets me up out of my seat, and then he tries the doorknob and it's open and he peers downstairs and shines his flashlight down there and I can hear the claws of those mangy dogs moving across the floor down there and they move toward the stairwell, and I'm thinking maybe he shouldn't go down there because those dogs start to growling and whatnot and I'm thinking that maybe my brother should wait until the landpeople come home because he probably will get bit. My brother takes a few steps down there and I'm thinking he's crazy because those demon dogs are getting all moany and everything, but my brother apparently doesn't give a shit because he heads down there and I can hear him moving shit around and the dogs barking and carrying on and I'm thinking I should go down there with a kitchen knife or something, and I call down there and ask my brother what the hell is going on and I'm watching the front of the house because some headlights are raking the window and I peer out onto the street to see if it is the landlord's blue van and it isn't.

After a while my brother comes back up the stairs and his eyes are wide and unsettled and I'm like what happened? And he brushes past me and goes into the living room and drops into the couch. I ask him again what happened because the lights and power didn't come back on and he's not saying or doing anything in particular and then my mind starts to wondering what the hell happened down there. He tells me I'll never believe what he saw and he goes on and says it was the most disgusting, disturbing thing he's seen in his entire life and I'm like, what? What happened? And he tells me the place downstairs is the most disgusting thing he's ever seen. He tells me there are piles of dog fur and dust and dirt and it's like a floor but not finished or anything, it's like maybe cement, but maybe it's dirt and there's a bed in the corner but like a prison cot and a toilet, but not like a toilet with a door or anything just a bowl sitting in the middle of the room and that's it. No sink or fixtures or basin, just a blank toilet and I'm imagining that man who looks like a gnome sitting on the toilet taking a dump while his wife is in some cot in the corner drinking vodka, and it turns my stomach, and then my brother tells me the dogs look sick and mangy and malnourished and the place reeks of dog shit and there's urine on the floor and dog crap and piles of fur and dirt as if someone just swept it into piles and left it there, and I'm thinking about the fucked-up paintings in the hallway and it all makes sense and it's not a pleasant thought at all and I feel nauseated and then my brother says he will never be the same after what he's just seen and I'm glad that I didn't go down there.

As it turns out the breaker was right there in our kitchen on the inside wall, and my brother felt pretty stupid because he went downstairs and everything and it turned into this whole big thing and he has those images in his head now and probably thinks about the basement now and again when he's trying to get to sleep, and there was no need to go down there at all.

My brother works through the night and bangs out his assignment. The following morning someone calls from that place Quality Temps. My brother answers the phone and he tells me it's someone from Quality Temps calling for me and hands me the telephone, and I'm not really sure what to say so I press the button on the phone that says, end. My brother looks at me for a moment, then looks back at his laptop computer and tells me I'm a buffoon.

PARK SLOPE FITNESS

THIS NEW GYM OPENS UP DOWN THE STREET AND I'M THINKING I SHOULD JOIN BECAUSE I'M GETTING FAT. And the thing is I am not fat in the right places. I have tits like my dad and I have hips like my mom and that's where the fat is. The fat is in the wrong places, the worst places. I'm fighting a battle against my fat. It's me versus the fat. I don't eat much. It's beer. Beer is what makes me fat and I like drinking beer. I like a cold beer at the end of the day.

So, anyway, I join this gym and it's pretty silly. I mean all these people running on treadmills going no where is stupid, and the guys are all dressed up in ridiculous running outfits with pants that match the top that match the sneakers and the sweatbands, and they've never played a sport in their lives but they're dressed like they're a member of the NBA. It just kills me. It really does.

This lady who says her name is Lisa gives me my first session. It comes free with new membership, they tell me. They asked me when I wanted my complimentary evaluation. They said it's free to new customers. Then they asked me if I preferred a man or a woman and it seemed like an odd question and it doesn't really make a difference either way but I tell them a woman like I don't care either way, but I guess it should be a woman. Why not have a woman give me my complimentary evaluation?

Lisa is the person who is going to give me my evaluation and I'm thrilled that she is very cute and she is very fit and she's got beautiful black hair and soft eyes. We are going to spend the next hour together and this isn't upsetting to me. Well, I'm a bit bothered that I don't have proper sporting gear. I'm a bit bothered that I'm wearing cut-off army pants and a T-shirt from some benefit function or something. Anyway, this lady Lisa tells me she needs to determine my level of body fat and she's real sweet and if I were to say she was flirting with me it wouldn't be a lie. I'm thinking she's way out of my league and she is just being nice and maybe she's like this with everyone and she does address other folks in the gym in a very pleasant manner and I'm trying to determine if she's being extra sweet to me because she likes me or if she's like this with everyone.

Lisa takes this metal pincher thing and tells me she needs to pinch the area beneath my shoulder blade and says I can keep my shirt on or I can remove it. There's no way I'm taking my shirt off because I'm fat and I have tits, so I mumble something and leave my shirt on. Lisa pinches the fat on my back beneath my shoulder blade. She does this through my shirt that I decided to keep on so I wouldn't offend her. She writes some information on a piece of paper and then tells me the percentage of body fat I have and I can't gauge from her reaction if the amount of body fat I have is obscene.

Lisa takes me over to a machine that has weights on it and she lifts the bar and shows me how you are supposed to do it, how you should properly lift the bar that is attached to some weights. She asks me what I do for a living and I tell her I am a musician. She seems real interested so I go on about my band and all. She tells me she wants to come hear me play and she tells me she loves music and she says she loves to go hear bands play.

Lisa tells me she'd love to do something sometime and I'm caught off guard. Lisa is way out of my league. Girls like Lisa don't ask me to do something sometime. I tell her sure and she asks what the weekend is looking like for me and I tell her I'm not doing much, band rehearsal or whatever. Lisa says that Sunday is a good day for her, it is her day off.

She tells me she would like to do something on Sunday if I'm available. She writes her phone number on a piece of paper and we go on with our evaluation. She continues to flirt and smile at me and I'm really starting to like this new gym.

I think about Lisa when I get home and I look at the piece of paper with her number and it's just amazing to me that a girl like Lisa gave me her number, just like that.

I do the usual thing that you do when you get someone's number, you know, do you call that night? Do you let it marinate for a night or two? Do you call the following day? And so on, like that, until you're like, this is stupid.

I have a couple five or six beers and call Lisa around eight or nine. She answers the phone and there's a kid screaming in the background and I'm like, okay, she's got a kid. No big deal. She asks me if she can call me back and she does about an hour later and it's quiet now in the background and we talk. She doesn't mention the screaming kid and I don't ask. It is as if neither of us heard the wailing, hysterical child. She asks if we can still get together on Sunday. She tells me she'd really like to see me and I'm thrilled and try to act like I'm not, even though a girl like Lisa could really change your entire world. A girl like Lisa could really make you get yourself together. I'd really have to lose weight with a girl like Lisa, I'd really have to get my act together.

Lisa tells me that we could meet at the Marriot Hotel in downtown Brooklyn. She asks me if I know where it is and I tell her that I do. I tell her I've never been there but I've seen it. She tells me it's gorgeous inside and she tells me that "they" meet there and she'd love to see me there on Sunday. I'm not quite sure what she means but I assume she'll be bringing the screaming child and that doesn't bother me one bit. She tells me there is a room called the Murphy Room on the second floor and that's where we will meet. She tells me eleven o'clock is when we will meet at the Murphy Room.

I go to the Murphy Room at the Marriot Marquis in downtown Brooklyn and there's a sign on the door that says something about Jehovah's Witnesses and now it all makes sense. I continue down the hall toward a red sign that says exit. I push through the door and take the stairs to the ground floor and I go back home.

I wonder why she would do that. I wonder what to say to this lady named Lisa who tried to trick me into going to a Jehovah's Witness meeting. I understand now why she was flirting with me. I wonder how many other fellas she tricked into going to a Jehovah's Witness meeting. I wonder why she didn't just tell me what the deal was, why she wouldn't just tell me that she is a recruiter or whatever.

I leave a message on Lisa's voice mail and I tell her that something came up on Sunday last minute and I was unable to make the meeting. I say meeting because that's what the hell it was.

I see Lisa at the gym giving an evaluation to this other dude. He's some dude who is fat like me and he's winded on the treadmill and Lisa is encouraging him. I see her smiling that smile and going on with the fat dude. I can't take my eyes off them because I remember the looks I was getting from other dudes in the gym. Dudes who probably went to the Murphy Room like I did and were duped into a meeting and now I remember the looks and now I'm looking at the fat dude like people were looking at me. I'm waiting for Lisa to write down her number, I'm waiting for her to slip the digits to the fat dude. And the fat dude is smiling back and he's jovial and joking around and he is, like I was, amazed that this honey with the soft eyes is flirting with him and it's really making his day like it did mine.

Lisa passes by where I am perched on this machine, the machine she showed me how to use, and she smiles and asks how the band is doing and I tell her the band is fine and I smile back. She asks when we can get together and I tell her sure, yeah, we should get together and I tell her I'll let her know when my band is playing and she knows and I know that she's never coming to see my band.

15 or 20 Minutes

THIS GUY IN THE NEXT ROOM IS SCREAMING IN HORROR. I've never heard anything like it. Maybe in the movies, but this is some real shit. Terrifying wailing and this whole entire thing sucks. And then there's this other voice I can hear kind of booming through the walls, a lower voice that is talking in normal fashion, and I can't make out what he's saying, but it sounds deliberately calm and reassuring. But that other guy, he's letting it all out, and it's quite unsettling. My hands were already numb and shaking but now they're moist, numb, and shaking, and I hope I'm not having a stroke or something because I've heard that those are the signs that you're having a stroke, your hands get numb and everything. I think it's the guy who was sitting across from me in the waiting room at this outfit called Dr. Monroe's office. It's a place you can go get an AIDS test, and they give you the results right there. None of this waiting for a week to get a slip of paper that's going to tell you you are going to wither away and die some lonely death in a beat-up apartment in the Bronx. I'm certain that that's what's going to happen to me because I've dreamed about it, where I'm sure I have AIDS and I knew it, I just knew that I'd be in that percentage. A billboard in Brooklyn said something about one in five people will have AIDS, and I'm that one in five. I've definitely got it.

The guy in the next room is still crying and weeping, and it's horrifying and I feel horrible. I was just sitting across from him in the waiting room pretending to be interested in *Family Circle Magazine.* He thumbed through *Time Magazine,* and then another guy came in a little out of breath and whatnot and the two of them kissed on the lips and those are the guys that are in the next room, and I'm thinking the guy that was there first is the one who is bawling and the reassuring voice guy is either Dr. Monroe or the guy who was out of breath. I mean what do you say to someone who has got AIDS? Dr. Monroe's job sucks. I wonder how many times a day he has to look at someone and tell them they're going to die. I guess people are living with AIDS and taking drug cocktails like Magic Johnson or whoever, but Magic is Magic, and most folks probably can't afford the drugs he gets and probably will die and shrivel up in a lonely existence. That's definitely what's going to happen to me because Dr. Monroe is probably minutes away from delivering my fatal blow. He's going to be the reassuring voice and I'm going to lose it, I can just feel it.

I found this ad on the back-page of *The Village Voice* a few weeks ago when I first noticed that my penis was red and

shedding skin on the underside. And I knew what it was
from. This one lady named Claire invited me over one night,
and she cooked me some stir-fry and we ate it, and then we
had a few glasses of red wine and talked up on her roof, and
she's cute and a few years older than me and has this
tremendous body. Anyway, we took a walk down to the
waterfront in Brooklyn and you know, we kissed and all that
and climbed up into this boat that was docked, and then she
pushed me onto my back and unzipped my trousers and all,
and then we continued this business up in her loft apartment
because her roommate was away. Claire had some weird
unfinished tattoos on her arms and back that looked like
they were scribbled by a third-grader. They made no sense
and I didn't really ask her about them and she didn't really
say anything about them, but I was thinking there was a
time when she got them and they probably seemed cool or
maybe she, like, spent time in jail or something or had some
previous shady existence down in New Orleans where she
said she was from. She was an oddball, this one lady. She
also had this weird cat that kind of appeared out of nowhere
and while we were flailing away with our business the
stupid thing was sitting on a chair watching us and I was
like get the heck out of here, but the cat was just perched
there watching us in bed. I didn't say anything to that lady
about being disturbed by the freaky cat because that'd seem
kind of weird, so I just every so often looked over there and
frowned at it and tried to make some terrifying face to make

it get the hell out of there, but the thing couldn't care less about what I thought and was obviously a voyeur. It wasn't helping me conduct myself in bed, that's for sure, so I launched a pillow at the cat when Claire went to use the bathroom, but the stupid pillow knocked over a bunch of crap on the nightstand and then I felt like an idiot cleaning up a bunch of candles and a jar of potpourri that got smashed on the floor, and had to give Claire some lame excuse about how all her stuff got knocked over and why there was shattered glass all in the floorboards.

Anyway, we continued with our business and I remember thinking that I have to remember the brand of rubbers I was using because it wasn't like other times when you felt as if you were doing it in a dream because it felt good but not that good because your penis is in a rubber glove. This time it felt great and these rubbers I'm definitely going to have to purchase again. After we finished with what we were doing I laid down on my back and went to pull the rubber off and I realized why it felt so good, the damn thing was still up in her or else got pulled off at some point. So basically I did what you're not supposed to do, and now I know why it felt great. You're supposed to use a condom, no matter what. One in five don't, and one in five get burned and I know it's me because now the underside of my penis is red and chaffed. That lady Claire didn't ask me to use a condom so I wonder if she doesn't use them because she has AIDS from when she was in jail down in New Orleans and probably doesn't care anymore because she's going to die, so why not take me with her. I pulled one out and she wasn't like some ladies who put the damn thing on for you to make sure it's on right—no, Claire told me she was on the pill and then I felt all stupid like, what am I supposed to do now? But then I looked at the jailhouse tattoos and I put the thing on anyway. So now it's up in her and that cat is looking at me like I'm a fool.

I get up and rush to the bathroom and find some serious liquid soap that says something about Dr. Bronner's cleanser or whatever. I lather up my unit and all around there and I'm making a mess in the sink but I think you can wash AIDS off if you get to it right away. I found out that that Dr. Bronner's stuff is some menthol cleanser that you really shouldn't be putting on your penis because my dick feels like it's on fire and gets all puffy red like it's pissed off, and it takes a good day or so before it gets back to a normal size and doesn't burn to high hell when I take a leak.

After a few days of the seriously burned penis I called an AIDS clinic and asked all kinds of dumb questions like, can you wash AIDS off after you've had sex? And the lady on the other end of the line acts like she's heard that question before and she tells me that most times AIDS is carried in semen or in the liquid of a woman's vagina and can travel through broken skin and I feel stupid because I probably washed the AIDS into my penis with that menthol stuff that opened up all the pores on the skin of my penis, and I'm the one who put the AIDS in there.

Dr. Monroe asks me if I've been practicing safe sex and I lie and tell him yes, definitely. I always practice safe sex, I tell him. I thought about telling him the story about the lady with the jailhouse tattoos but my voice was shaking uncontrollably and the lights in the room seemed so damn bright. Then he asks me if I've had multiple partners and I say something stupid like, at the same time? And he looks up from his clipboard and tells me it could be, but he asks if I've had intercourse with more than one person in the last year, and I tell him a few, so he asks more than five and I tell him no, not in the last year, and my voice cracks because there goes that number five again, I'm the one in five. He then asks when was the last time I was tested for HIV? I tell him it was a few years ago since the time my physician gave me an HIV test when he did my blood work, even though I told him I didn't want to wait a few weeks to find out if I'm going to die.

Dr. Monroe clasps that rubber band thing around my arm, pokes a needle into a vein and then takes a blood sample in a little vial, and then tells me he will have the negative results in about fifteen or twenty minutes. He exits the room and I sit and stare at the stupid clock on the wall that is not moving. I swear the minute-hand has moved once in the last ten minutes, which feels like a week, and now the wailing in the next room has turned to sobs. Soft muffled sobs, and then he starts with the no, no, no, no, no's. Those are bad. They go on for like an hour. NO, no, no, no, no, he says, and I start wondering how I'll break down. Will I wail uncontrollably and then go into the no, no, no's? I don't even have anyone to calm me down. That's sad. I'm going to die alone and broke and I'll never be able to have sex again. That lady Claire really should have told me she had AIDS. I think I've heard about people with AIDS being sent to jail for having unprotected sex with people and not telling them. That sucks what she did. She basically killed me. She murdered me by not telling me about the AIDS. She deserves to go back to jail.

The doorknob to my waiting room twists open and my heart shoots through my skull. Dr. Monroe comes in all somber looking and purses his lips. He looks down at a clipboard and says the word negative to me. I knew it. Negative news. He then asks me if I have any more questions and smiles at me. Negative? I ask and he tells me yes, the results were negative. You're fine, he says, you didn't test positive. Oh, I say and I try and act like of course I didn't test positive, even though I'm ninety percent sure I peed myself. I'm a little annoyed that he didn't just come in and say you're not going to die; the whole negative-positive thing is way too confusing when your brain is throbbing. The wailing in the next room starts again as I jump from the table and head toward the door. Keep doing what you're doing, be safe, Dr. Monroe says to me, and I detect a slight nod of his head to the wailing in the next room. I turn and go into the waiting room and see all the people awaiting their fate. The couples, the single men, all on edge, all pretending to read *Family Circle* or whatever. I sense them taking me in quickly, and I try not to smile, especially because the wailing from the guy spills out into the waiting room when I open the door and everyone's jaw drops upon hearing that. I mean that is not what you want to hear when you're going to get an AIDS test and you're thinking about that one time you were drunk or whatever and had unprotected sex, you do not want to hear someone in the next room wailing and going no, no, no. The receptionist smiles at me like this is business as usual and I head out the door and sprint into the south side of Central Park. I'm not going to die, at least not yet.

MISSY

MY MOM'S CAT TRIED TO BITE ME. I give up. I'm just not going to take the damn thing to the vet, that's all. Whatever. I'll call them and cancel, that's that. It's my day off and I can't be bothered with this. I don't have time for this and I'm not going to spend my entire morning trying to get the damn cat inside that stupid cage thing.

I call my mom and tell her I can't get her cat into the cage and I say it all quick and brisk and matter-of-fact as if I were telling her I couldn't unclog my shower, and she tells me I need to be more aggressive and firm in my tactics. She says it like she wants to encourage me and be all understanding and everything.

I did what my mom told me to do. I set the stupid cage out on the living room floor the night before I have to put the cat in it. She tells me to do this and she tells me it will make the cat unafraid somehow, like the cat will get used to the cage and not be intimidated. I think the cat is afraid, and I think the cat is brooding over the cage that's been parked in the middle of my living room floor all night. I'd be, I mean, if someone put a needle with an alcohol swab in the middle of my living room and thought I'd get used to the idea of a two-inch needle penetrating the fleshy part of my buttocks, they got another thing coming. I'd have a hell of a time getting to sleep thinking about the needle and the sting and my bare ass getting punctured. So, anyway, I leave the door open like my mother told me to do – as if the cat is going to crawl inside the cage and take a nap. I'm frustrated, annoyed, impatient, irritable, and I want my morning coffee in my café with my morning Post and I want to be about my business. I can't be bothered with this. It's my day off.

My parents had a house fire. Their toaster oven caught fire, or the socket that the toaster oven was plugged into caught fire, or something. They are staying at one of those Residence Inns, long-term stay type things and they can't have the cat there, so my mom asked that my brother and I keep her cat until they are able to move back into their house or whatever, or maybe my brother offered to keep the cat. Either way, I didn't offer. Not that I don't like Missy, it's just the cat box, you know, where is it going to go? I know my brother isn't going to clean the stink box because he doesn't clean anything and I'll end up cleaning it because I won't want the place to smell like cat crap when I have female company over because I can't stand when someone else's place smells like cat piss and I can't stand when you go into that person's bathroom and there's a cat box under the sink and the cat's in there and it's scraping around in that litter stuff and it just took a wet, pungent dump and it's a complete turn-off and it's like, do you really want to stay over with the cat up in your business and everything? And then the whole guy with a cat thing is strange too. I mean, if I were a woman what would I think of a guy with a cat? There are certain guys who have cats and then there's others who don't, that's all. You know, it's cute, I guess. Acceptable and admirable under my circumstances, you know, it shows some humanistic quality, my parent's had a fire and we're looking after the cat and all. But it's just not my style. That's the only way I can put it.

Anyway, my brother and I are arguing over where to keep the cat box and he suggests my bathroom because he wants to get me riled up. I tell him yeah, right, and suggest that we put it up in his room and he tells me, yeah, right. The kitchen is out of the question and we decide to put the kitty litter in our media closet because it has no door and is kind of in neutral territory in our apartment. Of course I'm the one who makes sure Missy has fresh water everyday, that her litter box is free of wet, stinky dumps and her food tray is kept free of dust balls. I'm the one who uses this rolling pin thing my mom gave us to extract Missy's fur from furniture, like our beds, the lounge chair, the couch, and the place mats on our dining room table, wherever she decides to take her naps. I like Missy. She's just fussy that's all.

I don't really get the sense in putting the cage thing out ahead of time because now Missy knows what's going on and she makes herself scarce. When I find her upstairs in the closet or under my brother's bed, or under the couch, or hiding in the bathroom upon seeing me, she begins yowling like some kind of demonic instinctual cry to let me know that anything goes homey, it's all fair game, you try and pick me up I'm liable to bite, scratch, do whatever, so long as I don't have to get inside that cage. I don't blame her. If it were me, I'd do the same damn thing. Who the hell wants to get inside some cage anyway? She knows it means one of two things - she's either going to the vet and is going to get shots, a Q-tip shoved in her ear, or some lady looking up her ass with a flashlight, or she's going to get groomed and she hates that. They even have to give her a sedative to comb through her matted knots of hair. This time out she's getting both, because she's walking around our apartment looking like a Rasta cat and her paperwork says she's due for her shots. She has to go to the vet. She has to get clipped and groomed. She has got to get her shots.

Missy is a Maine Coon. She has long, thick, grey, white, brown and black hair. Missy is arrogant, and Missy isn't at all playful, unless Missy feels like being playful. Everything is on her terms. When she feels like playing, she plays. This is how Missy is. Snobby.

My mother tells me to comb through Missy's hair every so often, and she leaves a comb and brush that sit idle next to her bag of adult food. When I pick up the comb Missy disappears and I just can't be bothered, so now she's got dreads and matted hair hanging off the scruff of her neck, around her backside and under her belly. She doesn't want me to do it, she wants to be left alone, and I don't blame her so I'm not going to do it, I'm going to leave her alone. I tell my brother to do it and he doesn't do what I ask him to do. He tells me to comb through Missy's dreads. So now someone else has to do it. Someone else is going to have to comb through her nappy, tangled hair, and she has to get inside the cage thing so I can bring her to the place where they will comb out her mess of hair and give her the shots she's due for. That's what's got to happen, there are no options here.

I get revved up this morning because Missy jumps off the couch that I asked her not to take naps on and scampers up into my brother's room. There's a big wad of matted fur on the couch where she was laying. I drop my shoulders in exhaustion. Her appointment is in an hour and I have to get her into the stupid cage and drive her over to the vet, which is twenty minutes away. I'm determined to do this. I talk to Missy and tell her that she doesn't have a choice, she has got to go to the vet and get her shots and get a comb out and I warn her that I'm not playing around and I try and act like I'm not scared of her, but it's that thing. That thing that's bothered me since I got tossed off that horse named Sasha at Ralph S. Mason sleep-away camp when I was eleven years old. Animals can sense fear, they told me. They told me that you have to act like you're in control. They warned that animals can smell fear. They said, get on the horse, yank the reins, kick the side of the horse in the ribs. Its big belly, its teeth that chomp through an apple effortlessly. This horse didn't want me on its back. The horse took off into the woods. They yelled, yank on the reins, kick its belly, yank on the reins. Sasha knew she was in control. They told *me* to be in control, to tug firmly on the reins, to let Sasha know who is the boss, take control. I thought I could make friends with Sasha and she wouldn't call my bluff and test the boundaries. I was terrified. I had to get on that horse. They told me I had to be aggressive, to not let them smell my fear. If they smell fear, that's it, they told me.

I tried to place myself in line so I'd get the little horse, the spotted one that looked like a pony or whatever, but I was huge for my age and they put me with the biggest horse in the entire barnyard. Big, aggressive, unpredictable Sasha. Sasha, who strayed off the path into the woods, rubbing close to trees, past branches that nearly took my head off. The lady kept yelling, yank on the reins, kick the belly with your heel. The kids laughed hysterically. My brother perched on his horse roaring with laughter. I was all red and flustered and wanted off, any way to get off the back of this living, breathing beast. I got my wish when Sasha lunged up into the air and bucked me up off her back and into the air I sailed, my arm twisted into the reins as she trotted further into the woods to graze. The hippy horse lady grabbed hold, freed my arm, admonished Sasha, and picked me up off the ground. Why didn't you yank the reins? she said. Sasha let a big pungent wad out her ass, her tail whipped back and forth and smacked me on the side of my face. Up you go, back up you go, other foot, then leg up and over, there you go, come on, the hippy horse lady told me. What's that saying that says something about getting back on the horse or whatever. Fuck that.

Missy, you're getting in that cage, get over here, I tell her. I yank her out from under my brother's bed and her head starts darting around, and her white pointed teeth snap at my hand and she runs past me downstairs. Goddamn it, the damn cat bites me. That's it, fuck that, Missy – forget it. What do I care? Fine. How could this little cat scare the shit out of me? You are such a wimp, I tell myself. It's a cat. You're a grown man. Cat. Man. Who is in control here? Put the cat in the box. Cat. Box. Put the cat in the box. It's simple.

Missy, get over here. Missy! That's it, I said. That's it, I don't care this time, you're getting in the box, is what I yelled. In.

The. Box. The cat bit me. Forget it. I'm not doing it. I don't have time to be dealing with this. Whatever.

I call my mom all frustrated but trying to act like I'm not frustrated and I just don't care about this because I have tons of other stuff to be dealing with in my life other than putting that cat in a box. I'm just like, it's just not worth the trouble of getting her, and putting her in the box. She doesn't want to go in the box so I'm not going to put her in the box. She bit me, I tell her. My mom tells me the cat is just scared, that's all. I need to get a blanket or something and throw it over Missy, wrap her up in it and pour her into the cage. That's what she told me to do, to pour the cat into the cage like a cocktail. I can't do it, she's not going to the vet, she's not getting groomed. She's not getting her shots. My mom says, okay don't do it, don't worry about it, because she knows how ridiculous this sounds and I'm a grown man and my life is a mess and this proves it because you can't even put the cat in the box for heaven's sake. You're not a grown man because you can't even do something as simple as put a cat in a box. Who can't do that? You put a blanket over the cat and pour her into the cage, what's the big deal? I'm not doing it, I can't be bothered with something as silly as putting a cat in a box, whatever, okay. My mom says, okay, don't put the cat in the box.

The phone rings. It is my brother. He doesn't even say anything, he's just laughing and he wants that I should tell him what happened because he wants to laugh more and he wants me to tell him the entire scenario and that's the last thing I want to do because I'm going to be hearing about this for days and I know he just got off the phone with my mother and she's telling him to encourage me to do it or whatever and this is just ridiculous at this point because it's turning into a whole thing and I don't have time to be dealing with this. I let him go on a bit and laugh, my ears burning and red because he just finds this hilarious and it's pissing me off and it is kind of funny but sad and pathetic because I'm like this grown man and I can't put the cat in the box and he's begging me to tell him what happened. He says, Missy bit you? Seriously, and his voice gets all normal. Seriously, tell me what happened, he says. I tell him that the cat bit me when I tried to get her out from under his bed, that's all, and he starts with the laughing again and I see Missy scamper past me. My brother tells me that I have to get her into the box. He's like you gotta do it, as if I don't have a choice. He tells me he'd do it but he won't be home until later and I have to do it, I have to get her into the box because she has got to get her shots and she has got to get groomed. It's not that big of a deal he says, just put the cat in the box. I tell him to forget it, forget about it. I tell him he's right, it's not that big a deal, so just forget about it, and he laughs even harder. I hang up because this conversation isn't going anywhere.

Her appointment is in a half-hour so I try and psych myself up as if I'm going into a bull fight, or I imagine it's the big game and I'm in the locker room. Let's go, let's go goddamn it, it's just a fucking cat, you're a human, a man can get the cat in the box, what's the big deal. I put an oven mitt on each hand because she can bite all she wants, she's going in the goddamn box. I don't have time to be dealing with this, it's a cat. I find her under the couch and I close the blinds because I look like this monster with the oven mitts on my hand and I put on a thick set of trousers and two sweatshirts so her fangs can't pierce through my clothing. Missy slips past me and slides across the wood floor and scampers up into my brother's room. Here we go again, and I'm yelling now and she's under the bed again and I pull on her leg and she goes hissing and all and bites me again and that's it, no more. Done. I toss the mitts on the floor and pick up the phone and I'm all flustered and salty and it's no big deal, she's just not coming in for her appointment and the lady on the other end of the phone asks that we keep the appointment because she's due for her shots and I lie and tell her I don't have a vehicle to transport the cat, and the lady on the other end of the phone tells me they can pick her up and tells me it's a service they provide because lots of folks in Brooklyn can't get their pets to the vet because lots of folks in Brooklyn don't have vehicles. The lady tells me they are sending someone to get the cat because I don't have a vehicle. Oh, I say, okay, and she reads me my address and I tell her that that's the address and I'm here and the cat is here and that's that.

I tell my mother that someone is coming to pick the cat up and my mom says, see I told you it would work out, and I just grunt.

This lady shows up after a while and asks where the cat is. She looks like a lady who does this type of thing, who picks up cats from people's houses out in Brooklyn. I tell her the cat is under the couch in the living room and she asks me what the cat's name is and I tell her the cat's name is Missy, and this lady is all calm because she probably does this kind of thing all day and it's no big deal to have some cat up under the couch and oven mitts tossed on a chair and a blanket here and the cage thing there, and this lady bends down and says Missy's name all pleasant like she's this little princess, and then she says it again like she's her best friend in the whole wide world, and then she pulls missy out from under the couch by the scruff of her neck, like you see mama cats hold their baby cats to move them from here to there, and this lady picks Missy up like that and says okay and is all reassuring and holding her how you're supposed to hold her and it's what I was supposed to have done but couldn't do because my life isn't on track and this is an example of my lack of courage and then I'm waiting for Missy to take a swipe at this lady and bite her like she bit me and I'm kind of hoping she does so I can say, see, that's what I was telling them about her biting and see, she bites, but the next thing I know Missy is in the box and didn't bite that lady, and the lady says, okay and closes the door to the box and says something about poopsies, then opens her hand to show a brown turd in her palm and then she tells me that Missy took a poopsie and how she's not going to worry about it until they get to the place where they're going to comb her out anyway. And I'm trying to act like it's no big deal either way, when it has been a big deal because my entire morning, or technically the past day has been spent trying to do what this lady did in less than a minute and I act as if I could have done what she did but I didn't do it because I didn't have a vehicle. I sign some paper that she puts in front of me and say goodbye to Missy, and Missy looks at me through the front of her box and she knows and I know that it was a big deal but, you know, whatever.

THAT ONE LADY FROM LA

THE F TRAIN BLOWS. Especially when it's 107 degrees down in the subway and it's like two in the morning and you're buzzed, but more like you've been buzzed but you're over it, and it's August, and you just want to go home and lay in bed with a pillow and listen to your fan bounce and creek and whirl in the window, blowing hot dusty air on your naked body because it's too damn hot to use sheets. The train is here and I'm sitting on it, but it's not moving because some dude is, like, dead beneath the train, someone says, and this spreads like wildfire and people start to fussing with bags and tossing looks around and sucking teeth all displeased and everything, and there are ambulances coming because some guy is like, dead under the train.

I get out the blasted train and I'm not interested in some dead dude, I'm pissed because the train conductor is making announcements into the intercom and it sounds like shit and it's loud as fuck and I'm trying to figure out how this could possibly be, how could he not know he sounds like he's got a fuckin' ham sandwich stuffed in his mouth and he's hollering through a backed-up sewer pipe. Some old stringy rocker dude with one of them black leather biker coats with straps and buckles and shit sticks an index finger in each of his ears and pinches up his face like a wrinkled prune 'cause the conductor is making that racket in the intercom and I'm trying not to look at the rocker dude's tight-ass pants and I'm thinking how ridiculous and out of place he looks 'cause he's packed into those jeans but he's probably coming from some rock show where everyone looks like him and wears jackets with all kinds of buckles and whatnot and ill-fitting jeans like it's no big deal.

The intercom feeds back atrociously and this composed man in a suit reminds me of when the train comes screeching like hell-fire into the station and the snobby people who try and act all calm and composed and ignore the sound like they're above it and unaffected, and how ridiculous it all seems because there is no possible way that noise couldn't piss you off to hell and back.

This irks me and I get out of the train all pissy and everything and I imagine a dude who shit his drawers and left them on his sweaty, festering ass for two days and then shit again and took a leak and this dude is sitting in front of me wearing a full-length wool coat and wool cap pulled down to his eyes and I'm thinking he's the one that I was thinking about because it smells like death and it's steamy, sweltering, funky-ass hot. I step out onto the platform and glance down on the tracks and there's a red sweatshirt ripped up under the steel wheels of the train and a dude's arm is where it shouldn't be, and the red sweatshirt is actually white in some places and in some places it's splotchy and I'm horrified to think that it's blood, and this is really not what I want to see and there are people looking and pointing and I'm thinking they need to mind their own goddamn business anyways.

I head up the stairs with all these other pissy folks and there's this girl who's got all kinds of bags and shit and she's struggling and no one's helping her 'cause they're all miffed because they have to transfer trains or whatever, and I take the bulk of the bags and help her, and when I get to the top of the stairs I look at her and she's fine, and I'm like, cool.

That lady I met briefly in the subway, the one who I helped carry unwieldy packages up the stairs for, gave me her number in Los Angeles. I call her after a couple days and leave my number on her voice mail. She calls me back all bubbly and she's got a sweet voice and because it's like three hours time difference she calls at nine o'clock her time which is twelve o'clock my time and she's like, are you in bed? and I'm like, yeah, even though I'm sitting in my living room watching that Richard Pryor movie *Stir Crazy* and I turn the volume down and my brother is like, what the fuck you doing? I toss him the remote and scamper into my room and slide the door shut and this honey from LA is telling me all she wants to do is get in the hot bathtub and how she bought all this lavender and sage oil and everything and I'm wondering if there's a reason she's telling me all of this business, and then while I'm thinking that, she asks me to hold on a second, so I do. I press the phone closer to my ear and I can hear a radio in the background and I'm trying to figure out what the heck is going on there. After a minute or so of this nonsense she comes back on the phone and says she needed both hands to take her dress off, and I tell her I wish I was there to help and I feel my face get all red and flushed and everything 'cause she could completely shut me down and say fuck off asshole and that'd be that, but it's not what comes out of her mouth and I'm pleased for this and that's all it takes, and next thing I know we're talking nasty and telling each other stuff that you tell someone when you want to talk nasty on the phone and it's late and your voice is all deep and you're trying to sound all sexy but it's really kind of ridiculous because if someone could hear you they'd laugh and be like, give me a break, especially if that person was my brother.

That lady from LA calls like every night and we talk. Nasty talk. She's freaky and it's pretty cool 'cause she can make me cum and she's like three thousand miles away and I don't have to make dinner plans at some overpriced restaurant that takes forever to feed me a lame portion, and put the toilet seat down, and call when I'm done with work, and put on some stupid dress shirt and pleated trousers to go out with her annoying friends and act like I like them and stuff and have them scrutinize my every move and then wonder what they say about me when I excuse myself to go to the bathroom. Nasty girl tells me in my ear the freaky stuff she wants to do to me, then she'd be like, did you finish? and I'd feel all stupid and be thinking about the nasty things she just said about licking my ass and the stuff I'd just said about doing the same to her and I'd be searching for something to wipe off on and I'd be like, no not yet, and she'd still be saying stuff to me about tonguing my balls, and I'd be like saying whatever and it'd go on like this for a bit until I had to take a wicked leak and knowing it'd be all loud I'd sit on the toilet so I could hit the side of the bowl and she'd be telling me she's cumming and be all moaning in my ear and I'd be praying my semi-erect penis doesn't hit the toilet water and then I'd be like, I'm cumming, and be all breathing in the phone. Nasty girl. Nasty boy.

After a month of this nasty business that lady tells me she's coming to Brooklyn to get nasty with me. In person. So I'm like, cool, bring it, nasty girl. And she tells me to get all the freaky stuff ready we had talked about, so I go to one of them freaky stores in Greenwich Village and buy the items deemed freaky from this freaky dude, with a piece of metal stuck through his tongue who wraps up my freakiness in a nondescript brown paper bag like he does all day. I want to peek inside the freaky bag while riding home on the F train but I imagine it all spilling out onto the floor and the looks I'd be the recipient of, so I put two steady hands on my nondescript brown paper bag sealed shut with a length of Scotch Tape, and look at all the people on the subway and all the bags they are holding and imagine the funky stuff people could be carrying and not looking at, for fear it will spill to the floor and the looks they'd get. And I feel thrilled that no one knows what kind of business is in my bag.

My freaky girl arrived on a Friday. I did a quick spray and wash and wipe down on the toilet, put fresh linens on the bed and cleared the next couple days of any responsibilities. I gave my brother a heads-up that this one lady was coming from LA to visit me. I even liked the way it rolled off the tongue - a freak from LA was coming to spend a long weekend.

She very conveniently got herself to my apartment in Brooklyn and said something about her sister who lived nearby and picking her up at the airport and whatever. I had dedicated my bedside drawer to the freaky business and was staring at the business when the doorbell rang. Nasty girl was here. I opened the door and she looked grand. I mean, LA girls are certainly well put together. A severe part was strategically chiseled into her hair over her left temple and the hair on either side of this part was pulled taut in either direction and disappeared somewhere behind each ear. She was better looking than I remembered, and her swift, nimble features were in proportion to her trim body. Her skin looked like porcelain with not a blemish. She had on one of them thin tailored leather jackets, and her perky breasts danced inside a purple angora sweater that matched her matte purple lipstick and whatnot. And then I felt weird - I mean, I felt like I didn't know who this person was and she knew all this business about me and told me she wanted to tongue my balls and whatnot and suddenly I wished we had never talked nasty. I wished she had just told me about college and her friends and where she grew up and places she'd traveled and people she'd met and stuff. But she didn't and we were already here and never went there. It was like waking up next to someone after having had drunk, incoherent sex the night before and seeing them in the light for the first time and feeling atrociously awkward.

That lady handed me a gift. It was a long cardboard poster tube and I imagined her maneuvering it through the crowded airplane and felt ashamed because I didn't get her anything - well, not really. I opened it. It was a laminated poster of the world. She leaned in and tongue kissed me and my back stiffened. I want to say that I saw skyrockets. That all my apprehension disappeared with that one kiss. That the weekend was as nasty as we talked about. But I can't. The taste of her breath was gingivitis. Clinical. Like old folks nursing home gingivitis. Like the kind that might emanate from a tenth-grade science teacher named Mr. Nelson, who wears the same v-neck sweater three times a week, and the collar of the white shirt that peaks out from the v-neck sweater has an ancient rust-colored ring around it, and no one wants to sit up close to his desk because his breath smells like ass, so there is a horseshoe of occupied seats arched away from his desk, and when you talk to your buddies in the back of the classroom and piss him off, he tells you to take the seat up front, and it's like the worst, and people are snickering in the back 'cause they know you're just dying up there with the breath and all.

Her teeth were pearly white but her breath was like a junkyard, which I found annoyingly absurd. I thought of all the nasty things she talked about doing with my man juice and about all the nasty things she must've done with other people's man juices. She was bisexual and I thought about all the nasty things she had done with other women's bodily fluids, the things she had told me she wanted to do with other females' anatomy with me as active participant.

Here's how our conversation went down:

What's the matter? she said to me.
Whattayamean? (*This girl eats other girls' butts*)
You pulled away.
What?
  Kiss me.
Then, a quick kiss.)
Are you freaked out?
No.(*This girl eats other boys' butts*)
It's okay.
I know.(*This girl told me she can eat her own butt*)
You are freaked out.

I'm – what do you want me to say?

It went on like this for five minutes, which seemed like hours as my mind raced to think up an escape route. Four days of this was unacceptable. What if I told her I was sick with the flu and we shouldn't kiss for fear she could catch my germs? What if I told her there was a family emergency and I have to leave immediately? I could get my brother in on it and everything.

She grabbed my genitalia and stroked me. Clearly she knew what to do 'cause I didn't want it to do what she wanted it to do, but it did it anyways and I was pissed at that flesh between my legs because it does what it wants to do whenever it damn well feels like it, and most times I feel like I'm just along for the ride because it's calling the shots even when I say no, and has a nasty habit of getting me into situations like the one I'm in.

I asked her all sensitive-like if we could take it slow. I figured a less aggressive approach might connect with her feminine sensibilities. So she kissed me like you do to reassure someone, you know, slow and all. Backfire. I kissed her neck and she smelled good, rich, clean.

I discovered how she achieved the disappearing act with her hair as a bobby pin loosened behind her ear. I didn't fix it, instead I put my lips near her ear and asked her if maybe she should, like, stay with her sister so we could take it slow, and as soon as I said that I wished I hadn't because that really pissed her off, and she shoved herself away from me and was all offended. She proceeded to find my liquor cabinet and pour herself a drink. Scotch in a Dixie cup, and didn't offer me one. She walked hard across the wood floor with her pointy boots and sat on the edge of the couch all stiff and started dialing numbers on the phone, jamming the buttons all hard and everything. I kind of disappeared into the back room and took a leak. I had bought some silly, smelly aromatherapy candle or whatever and had put it on the back ledge of the toilet and it sat there and mocked me, and I felt like smacking it to the floor.

After a while I carefully made my way across the creaky wood floors and appeared in the living room and she didn't even look up at me and the color of the booze in her Dixie cup was white and I saw that the Absolute Vodka cap was off. Wonderful. She shook her head and glared at the phone as if it had called her something vile and hateful, like cunt, and then she slammed it down on my brother's wood coffee table. I wondered if she had called a cab or what the deal was, but I felt like I should keep my stupid trap shut for a while and wait until I'm spoken to.

She began to mumble to herself and curse me to the room, and gesture and shake her head, all pinched up, and was looking the opposite way from where I stood, and was all pissed and said she had bought a plane ticket and came all the way from Los Angeles for this. Then she called me an asshole and I couldn't have agreed more. She said she didn't fly out here to stay with her sister and her stupid boyfriend in their crummy apartment in Brooklyn and she was trying to call friends in the city so she could leave but her friends weren't around and she was annoyed and I was annoyed at her friends, too. I hoped they'd be around soon, and was more than willing to gather up her belongings and facilitate a group move.

I caught a glimpse of her manicured hands, and the care and detail made me feel awful. Then guilt set in and I told her I didn't really mean what I said but I said it and you can't take stuff like that back. Then I wished I hadn't said what I just said again because that's what you call mixed messages and that's been known to get people pissed, especially someone who flew out from LA and can't stay where they were supposed to stay because this guy is acting stupid, and then you have to explain to your friends, who want to know why you called their cell phone ten times, that shit didn't work out with this asshole who lives in Brooklyn and says he plays drums in some band. Then she started to smile but it wasn't like she was happy or anything, it was one of them sneers like you're pissed, and you're not just going to sit there and take it, you're going to do something about it and you're thinking about what you're going to do and you're planning and you sneer, like this lady from LA was doing.

Then my brother came home and he's trying to be extra loud when he comes up to the door because he knows this lady from LA is visiting and she's freaky and we could be getting buck wild on the couch and whatnot. He poked his head inside the door and that lady from LA was on his couch with that sneer and whatnot and she gulped the remainder of her vodka and they shook hands and my brother was all polite and he had no idea what the hell was going on and why this lady was sitting on his couch all pissy and smelling like a goddamn liquor store and drinking his vodka, and why I'm standing in the other room looking all stupid and pathetic and not drinking. Then he glanced at the ridiculous poster of the world on the floor that was all unraveled and battered-looking because that lady had swiped it off the couch, and he tried not to smile because now he knows that shit ain't going right and he excused himself upstairs into his room and put on some jazz music, and I know he's up there just laughing his ass off because if it were happening to him, I'd be.

No one was calling her back so she started gathering her things and fussing with her crap, and I'm wondering what kind of business is in her little black weekender freak bag that rolls on wheels, and I feel bad because she had put together outfits and probably bought that lingerie she was talking about that she said was like a human sock with one hole in the right place, and I was all intrigued, and now it sat, folded and neat and unused inside this weekender bag, and I just wanted to start over and be friends and get her out of this funky mood, so I asked her if she wanted to get something to eat and she just said to the wall, where?

I took her to dinner at this out-of-the-way Mexican restaurant way over in the West Village and she drank some more. Tequila. Margaritas. Sangria. She sat sideways on her chair so she was facing anyone but me and she made eye contact with all kinds of folks, like the squat Mexican busboy who she asked what his name was and he told her, Pedro, and she said it a few times trying to get the accent right and roll her tongue and whatnot, and then he says it like you should say it and she says it again like it's a question so he'll feel obligated to repeat it correctly and say it all slow so she could get it right, but she was all drunk and her tongue wasn't cooperating and the other squat busboys were saying stuff to each other in Spanish and I knew, even though I couldn't understand them, that this was making their night because the hot drunk chick from LA with the perky breasts inside a purple angora sweater was going on and on with their boy Pedro and they were trying not to smile, especially when their boss, who looked like Gary Busey with a shock of white hair, and thick lips, and teeth too big for his mouth came around the corner and shot them a look as he wiped down two plastic menus and set them in front of us. They got to looking busy real quick, fussing with water glasses and yellow corn chips that baked under a heat lamp, and when Pedro came over to them to refill our chips they whispered stuff to him in Spanish, and that lady was just having a ball starting shit and making me look like a buffoon, so I went to the bathroom and looked at myself in the mirror and my ears were all flushed and red.

The lady who brought my Nachos Grande to the table was dressed in this ridiculous fluffy, flowery dress like Mexican ladies should be wearing and her hands had that scaly shit on them, I think they call it eczema or psoriasis, or whatever, and it's really hard to look at, especially when it's on the hands and arms and elbow of your food handler, and I'm wondering why she's near any food in a restaurant in the first place. I wish I worked for the city or something and I could flash a badge 'cause I'd shut this joint the fuck down, and I'm hoping she's not touching my Nachos Grande and I'm watching her thumb on the up side of my plate and the thumb has some of that crap on it and it's red and scaly and the nail is worn down to a nub and I'm bummed out because even though I don't have a serious appetite I need to eat something, and I don't want that scaly shit on my lip in the morning and I'm thinking she should be wearing gloves or something or, like, taking the night off, and now Pedro is filling my water glass and that lady from L.A. is carrying on with him and ordering another margarita, and the lady with the red nub asks me if I want another Sprite and I say no, all quick and stuff, because the entire weekend is a bust and I'd like to wrap this whole thing up quickly and get back to my life.

So I'm picking at my Nachos Grande and I'm burrowing to the bottom of the pile because I think the scaly crap didn't get down there and that one lady goes to the bathroom without saying shit to me, like I'll be right back or whatever, and she's gone for a while and I'm thinking she's booting up her Fajitas that came to the table with all kinds of smoke and charcoal and noise and fanfare, and I'm like, fuck, because if she's all shit-faced and vomiting where does that leave me? I crank my neck and all the squat busboys are looking at me like you look at someone when you know something they don't know and you'll probably know it soon, like when you pull into a rest stop and have a flat tire and don't yet know it and the dudes in the next car over are watching you climb out of your car and are all in your business and saying shit to each other and waiting to see the look on your face when you see what they see when they should be minding their own business anyways.

Now I see what they see, and I now know why they're looking at me like I got a flat tire, because that lady from LA is in the bar area near the bathrooms where it's, like, Fiesta Night or whatever, and people are carrying on and she's carrying on with them and there's Mexican music and waitresses in them stupid frilly dresses and big screen televisions showing a soccer game, and Pedro comes over and asks me if I'm done with the eczema nachos with the napkin laid across the plate. I flick my hand at him without making eye contact because he's not cool, and I should tell Gary Busey that he's a pain in my ass and if I was a waiter, or busboy or whatever he is, I wouldn't be carrying on with some dude's date gone bad.

I'm thinking I should just split, and leave like eighty bucks on the table and hightail it out of there when that lady comes stumbling around the corner, probably because she's thinking I'm thinking that and isn't going to let me off easy, and her creased hair is no longer creased and it's sad because she's coming undone.

We walked down Bleecker Street, which was a really bad idea, but wasn't my idea because I'm just kind of following her, and she's like ten feet in front of me all drunk and shit and she dips into this crowded bar and I'm standing outside this enormous fogged-up window that says some Irish name in gold letters like Mahoney's or McGuinn's or something, and I ask someone if they know the time, and that someone tells me it's nine-thirty, and I can't think of a time when I've been less thrilled to hear that sequence of numbers. People are out and carrying on and it's really mild out and it's Friday night and they are on dates and out with friends and it's still early and everyone is drinking and smoking, and it's their big night out and they're dressed up in creased slacks, and lipstick isn't yet smeared and hair is in place, and crisp shirts are tucked in and it all pisses me off, especially when I go in the crowded bar that smells like vinegar and piss and that lady's hair is all fucked up and the outfit that looked well put together is starting to come undone and she's drinking shots with two guys who are all big and East Coast and looking to pick chicks up, and you can tell because they are wearing brightly colored button-down shirts and pleated khakis with canvas belts, and I'm sure they smell like Polo aftershave and they're wearing penny loafers with no socks or whatever and here's this hot chick who is drunk and it's like a total score and it's only nine-thirty.

Then I'm pissed because she doesn't leave with one of the guys with the pleated khakis who looks at me and wonders why this girl that I am sort of with is carrying on with them and standing all close and flirting, and they're probably thinking she's too loaded and sloppy drunk, and they're weighing options and thinking about if it's worth it to get caught up with her, seeing that it's only nine-thirty and other chicks are filing into the loud, vinegar-piss, Irish bar.

I try to make my face look as sour as possible but she seems to like me to look pissed so I try to look like I don't care and she stumbles over and hands me a flat beer in one of them pint glasses, and I take a sip and it is flat and stale and tastes like pooh. I realize that even if she did leave with one of these Polo guys her crap is at my house, and I get to thinking that I should've never helped her carry her packages up the stairs in the subway. Then I feel like a heel because everyone was looking and laughing and gesturing at her and then they'd look and laugh and gesture at me and wonder why this hot girl with her arms folded was so angry and what could I possibly have done to piss her off, and then I wonder if I should drink heavily too, and just forget everything, the breath and all, but it's too late and she is too drunk and we are heading down a completely different road. No turning back.

Could I leave her there on the street, ruining her well thought out LA outfit as she sits plopped down on the street corner of Fourth Street and Seventh Avenue South? No. Because if something happened to her, like if she got hit by a car or if some asshole raped her, it would suck and it'd sort of be my fault having encouraged her to come from LA and get all dolled up. A cop swung a glance in my direction. You know the glance that says he's really too tired and not too much in the mood and his shift is probably over in forty minutes and he just wants to go home and stuff, but if he wanted to he could be in the mood and not be tired and it'd ruin your night that looks pretty sad anyways, but it'd really suck to get your hands bound behind your back by zip ties and sit in the back of a police car looking all pathetic and stupid and then get put behind bars with fines and fees and bail and whatnot, so I decided to get the dame up off the corner of Seventh Avenue South and Forth and get her to shut her trap. I hoisted her rag doll body to her feet and she made it so she'd fall if I let go, so I had to like hold her up and stuff, which was pretty awful and looked ridiculous. Then she began cursing me to the world. Loudly. Telling passersby how much of an asshole I was. Which I fully admitted to her, but I didn't see the necessity of letting every Tom, Dick and Jane in on it.

I propped her next to a mailbox and hailed a cab and it's a pain in the ass to get a cab to drive you to Brooklyn anyway, and when you have some fucked-up broad with you it's nearly impossible. After two or three attempts I finally get a cab to not pull away after they digest my absurd situation, and I shove that lady from LA in this cab and she just tumbles to the floor and the taxi driver digs his eyes into the rear view mirror 'cause that lady is hollering about something or other and her shirt's all up her back and her ass crack is coming out the back of her three-hundred-dollar designer jeans. I tell the driver that we're going to Brooklyn, just over the bridge I assure him, and he tosses a look in the rear view mirror and I try to look as confident as possible. I notice his tags declare that his name is Mohammed Mohammed, and he asks me if she's okay and I feel like saying to him, what the fuck do you think? But before I say anything the lady from LA tells Mohammed Mohammed that I'm an asshole and Mohammed hits the meter and pulls from the curb.

We almost reach DeKalb Avenue when she pukes a vile mess all over the seat, floor, and door of Mohammed's cab, and Mohammed yanks the car to the curb and is all pissed and I don't blame him. I pass Mohammed some money through the divider and quickly shove that lady out onto the sidewalk just as her mouth makes a big o and there's a stream of fajitas and beer and vodka and golden brown chips and sangria and salsa and scotch and kamikazes and wine exiting deep from her bowels like a fire hose. My sneaker is brown with this vomit and I'm thinking it could've been worse, but then when the smell of her puke hits my nose I start to doubt it. I let her use my coat to clean up and now she's all quiet but not really humiliated like she should be and I'm praying she's not getting a second wind because if she is I think my conscience will allow me to ditch her and let fate takes its course, but the last thing I need is, like, her sister and her stupid boyfriend calling and showing up at my house and telling me that her sister was gang raped by some fourteen-year-old punks from Bay Ridge.

I asked that lady where her sister lives and she told me she doesn't know, which couldn't have been farther from the truth, and I knew it was somewhere in Fort Green so I steered us in that direction, and homeboys on the corner out in front of bullet-proof glass Chinese restaurant windows were all staring and saying shit and whatnot, so I eventually had to get a livery car to take us back to my house before we got jacked the fuck up.

I dumped her rag doll body in my bed and set a bucket nearby. I thought about her pulling a Hendrix and vomiting in her sleep and dying and thought that'd suck, so I kind of kept watch of her so there wouldn't be an ambulance out front and my brother coming downstairs in his skivvies all annoyed and everything.

She woke up around eight in the morning and I had a glass of water and some aspirin ready and we both thought it best if she left. She apologized for her behavior and was embarrassed and all but I didn't really care, I deserved what I got. I told her it was me, not her. I was the asshole and I didn't blame her for being upset. She didn't really like that, but we politely kissed goodbye anyways. I wondered what other people thought when they kissed her. Was it possible she was unaware of her foul situation?

I removed the contents of my bedside drawer and put the lot of it back in the nondescript paper bag and shoved it in the side pocket of my laundry bag.

That lady from LA never called again and I kind of miss our conversations. Not the phone sex but just having someone three thousand miles away. Someone I could talk to at the end of a long day. No commitment, no boyfriend-girlfriend drama, just a voice at the other end of the phone.

BY THE POUND

BY THE POUND IS WHAT MY GUY ON THE CORNER CALLS HIS BUSINESS. IT'S A BUSINESS THAT DOES YOUR LAUNDRY BY THE POUND SO IT MAKES SENSE THAT THAT'S WHAT HE CALLS IT. I've been going to him for over a year since I decided it probably costs the same amount to have these folks do my laundry as it does for me to do it myself. Maybe a few more dollars, but I don't have to sit in some stupid Laundromat watching the lights on the washer go from spin cycle to dry cycle to clean cycle, and then keep opening these oversized dryers and paw around in my laundry for what's wet and what's moist and what's dry so I can wean out items that are done from the ones that still need more dryer time. It can take an entire afternoon of my day and people are all in there in what's left of their wardrobe, like that time I had no clean underwear and was in there freeballing in a pair of ill-fitting cotton sweatpants that were just embarrassing. There's nothing fun about doing your laundry. It's a pain in the ass, especially when folks bring a gangload of kids in there and it turns into a daycare center with kids hollering and pushing laundry carts over your feet and carrying on while their moms watch Jerry Springer or some dumb reality show or the show that really gets on my nerves—People's Court—or that lady Judge Judy who is always making a fool of some chump who is lying about this or that and his ex-girlfriend who hands some documents to a court clerk who's trying to act all professional and dry and serious and passes those documents to that lady Judge Judy who is always tearing into somebody about their crummy life and asking them how could they do something so stupid and telling them to shut up when they try and answer her question, and the folks in the Laundromat are watching it like it's some real thing and go uh-huh, uh-huh, and whatnot, like they have nothing better to do, and going on and on with the uh-huh's like they have never done anything dumb in their lives, and it just seems stupid that people pay attention to these shows and waste good time staring at the television set, and I wish someone would put on ESPN so I can catch some scores, but that never happens.

Anyway, my guy, the guy on the corner, does a great job with my wash and everything comes back stacked perfectly and folded nice, so nice that most of the time I don't even bother putting it away. I just live out of the laundry bag. My guy who owns the place is really friendly and knows me and he knows my brother and he always greets me with a big smile and asks about my band and he gets a kick out of the fact that I play drums and whatnot, and I like him even if he might be putting on a show of it all. It doesn't bother me one bit. Recently he got a new hairstyle, my guy who told me his name is Joe, even though I bet he's got some cool Chinese name that he thinks is hard to pronounce by us stupid Americans. His new hairstyle is a bit weird, a bit off-putting. He's got it curly like an Afro and he's got blond highlights on the ends and it's kind of weird, but if he likes it I'm cool with it. I try and pretend to not notice it at first but he's just beaming behind the counter waiting for me to say something, and I can tell he's all excited to talk about the hair and so I tell him I like his hair even though it's weird, the new hairstyle.

I haul my duffel bag down to him a couple times a month or so and I see him almost everyday when I pass by his storefront on the way to the Manhattan-bound D train that is right next to his shop. He waves, and his wife smiles and waves, and they've got a teenage son and then a daughter that's in college and she's just perfect and cute and she's extra friendly to me, but I know she's probably like that to everyone and every so often I see her at the bodega across the street getting this or that when I'm getting this or that. I thought about asking her to one of my shows but this one time I was in that bodega getting these condoms and she came in behind me so I'm trying to hustle Manny, the guy behind the counter, up, but he's not doing that, he's going on in Spanish to his boy, Jesus, who is in the back, and the condoms are sitting on the counter with a forty-ounce of

Budweiser. And Shin Lee, the daughter of my guy who owns By the Pound, comes up to the counter so I grab the condoms all quick and accidentally knock them on the floor, and she looks down and I swipe them up real fast and it's pretty embarrassing because the box says Magnums, and I try to cuff them in my hand before Shin Lee sees, and then I give Manny the money all quick and matter of fact but I'm pretty sure she saw the Magnum condoms. She probably thinks I have somebody and she's probably too young for me anyway, but I like Shin Lee and I like her folks and her teenage brother.

Well, things got mucked up with my guy on the corner because my laundry bag is there and I haven't picked it up in over two weeks and I've run out of underwear and I need to get in there and get my freshly laundered items that they fold all nice and neat. I've been washing the last pair of underwear I own in my bathroom sink and drying it on the shower rod, but now I need my clothes and I'm thinking of asking my brother to pick my stuff up and that'd just be stupid because he'll be like, why don't you get it yourself, and I don't really feel like telling him why he should haul my big bag of clean laundry down the street, so I don't. I don't because if he knew why I wasn't picking up my laundry there's no way he'd go get it either, and then he'd be laughing at me and bothering me about picking up my laundry, and he'd be laughing at the ridiculous clothes I'm wearing and going on and on about it, so there's no way I'm asking my brother, and there's no way I'm telling him the real reason I'm not picking up my wash.

My guy's wife has seen me pass by in the morning going to get the train and I walk by all quick like I'm in some big rush, and I've pretended to be on the phone on some important call and she looks at me from behind the counter and I'm not certain, but I'm pretty sure I saw her make a face at me this one time. I'm almost positive she shook her head and frowned and I'm not sure if she's pissed off or if it was a frown of disappointment. The thing is, the train stop is right next to By the Pound and there's really no way to avoid passing by unless I walk ten minutes out of my way down Flatbush Avenue to the Atlantic Avenue train station. A few days ago my brother picked up his laundry and Joe told him my bag was ready and asked that I come pick it up. My brother told me they told him to tell me to come pick up my bag and I tell my brother that I will. I tell him not to worry about it, I'll get my wash, and my brother looks at the mismatched socks that I'm wearing and the trousers that are too tight, and he pinches his face.

It's not that I don't want to pick up my bag or I don't have the twenty or twenty-five bucks to pay for it, I actually do. I've got the money. Here's the thing that happened. What happened was my parents came over to stay at our flat for the weekend, and because I have like a queen size bed or whatever my folks stayed in my room so I did what you do when your folks are going to stay over—I hid all my paraphernalia, like my pipes and lighters and bong and all that. I hid all that in the side compartment of my duffel bag that serves as my laundry bag. Well, that stuff wouldn't have been so bad, the real problem is I hid all that freakiness from my freaky weekend in the side compartment and it's stuff that will certainly make the nice family from By the Pound question me and my lifestyle or whatever, because the stuff that was in there is like nasty stuff. I don't even want to get into it, but it's stuff that's keeping me from picking up my wash; it's stuff that makes me practically run past the storefront in the morning, but now I really need to get my wash because my entire wardrobe is down there and I'm walking around dressed in a concert T-shirt for Pearl Jam that barely touches my belly-button and has paint all over it because I used it as a smock when I painted my folks' house, and I have on a pair of green cotton trousers that are for a suit that I haven't worn in years because there's no room in the groin, and I've been washing the same damn pair of underwear in the sink for over a week. This is what's going on, this is the way things are.

So now I'm casing the joint, I'm across the street clocking By the Pound so I can time it when maybe the dad is behind the counter by himself and not the daughter, Shin Lee, who I like, or the mom, Lucy, and now it's turned into a whole thing and I'm trying to get the nerve up to just go in there but there's like a double-sided dildo and crap in the side compartment of my laundry bag, and there's no way they didn't see all the sex oil and the porn DVDs and the handcuffs and whatnot. They definitely saw all of it and that's just embarrassing. I know the wife and daughter do the laundry so it was definitely one of them that found the stuff and I'm sure they probably dug around in there thinking it was dirty clothing because I have stuffed socks in the side compartments when I'm jam packed in the main portion of the bag and they've got them out and washed them. I hope it was the mom who found the stuff, I guess, because she probably found it and shoved it back in and most likely didn't make a big fuss because she pretty much keeps to herself and most likely she didn't feel the need to make a big production out of it and show it to Joe, and I can't think of a reason she would show it to Shin Lee unless she was like see, don't ever trust him, he's a pervert and no good. I definitely hope Shin Lee didn't find all the porn and whatnot because there was some porn in there that was nasty and was like mega porn and there was porn that was all Asian girls and I don't have a fetish or nothing, it was just part of the four-for-ten series. I'm not one of those guys that just digs Asian girls like my friend Brad who is all into Asian girls but it's like embarrassing because we could be out somewhere and he'll start talking Thai or Burmese or something to an Asian woman and picking them up right there on the spot and asking for their number, and he gets the numbers but it's still weird that all he thinks about and all he dates are Asian women. I remember this one time me and Brad were taking a flight to Los Angeles and they did a bag check on him at the security gate and half of his carry-on bag was stuffed with dirty magazines and all the magazines had naked Asian women on the cover and had names like *Orientail* and had some naked Asian woman bent over showing her butt. That was embarrassing but the strange thing was Brad wasn't embarrassed at all; he was more concerned about the lady rifling through his stuff and pawing at his mags, and he even commented like, careful that one's my favorite, and I was embarrassed for him but he couldn't care less. I'd be embarrassed to no end to have Shin Lee find that stuff and be like, he's a pervert, or look at me funny and tell her friends about the guy she liked who has an Asian fetish so she got totally turned off. That'd just kill me.

So, anyway, that's why I'm pacing around on the other side of the street from By the Pound and going on and up the street like some private eye trying to time this whole thing perfectly so I don't have to face Lucy or Shin Lee. I could probably deal with Joe or Kim, the teenage son—them I'm not as concerned with because I'm sure they'll just think it's normal, because guys, we do watch porn, I mean I go to some porn websites and it's like millions upon millions of people watching it and downloading it and I've heard that the most bandwidth used in the world is for porn. Pornography is what is flying through the air beamed by satellites but it's still not what you tell people about, you keep that stuff under wraps and it's not what you want people, especially a cute girl named Shin Lee, to know about.

It's definitely the double-sided dildo that's keeping me across the street but the mega Asian porn is just about as bad. It'd really be embarrassing if the mega Asian porn was found by Shin Lee. What if I come in and Joe yells at me and goes on about disrespecting Asian women. And what if other people who live on my block, who I know go to By the Pound, are in there when Joe yells at me and what if Lucy, the mom, breaks down or throws something at me? My whole neighborhood could definitely turn on me even though the guys probably watch mega porn but they don't let the whole world in on it, they don't leave it in a laundry bag for their guy and his family to find, but that's what I did.

When I finally get up the nerve to go inside By the Pound, after I'm certain I timed it so just my guy, Joe, will be in there shutting down for the night, Joe is back there doing stuff, and then the mom, Lucy, pokes her head out from back where the washing machines are, and I see a back door that I knew nothing about, but now I do know, now I know there's a back door and my whole plan is blown. Then this lady Jane comes in with her twin kids in one of those high-end strollers that are ridiculous, and then Kim, the son, comes out of the bathroom and it's just a damn party in there. And I can tell they've found the perverted stuff. I can tell because they all look at me, and they never all look at me at the same time, but that's what they do, they look at me and they look at my ridiculous trousers and the dumb shirt I'm wearing, and I'm all sheepish and I approach the counter all shy, and I'm sure my face is, like, burning red and I do something stupid like wave, and Joe says something real quick in Chinese to Lucy, his wife, and she says something quick back, and they are both sneering at me because they found all my stuff in there. The freaky stuff. The mega Asian porn and the double-sided dildo, and there was all kinds of stuff in there, and the least of my worries is the pipe and the one-hitter—that, I couldn't care less about—it's the handcuffs and all, the stuff that makes me look like some freak. Joe smiles at me like he usually does but there's something different about that smile, and I'm freaking out and my hands are all sweaty, so I let Jane go first because her kids are making a racket and because I don't want them to yell at me and have her be a witness to my demise. Jane finally leaves and I pay for my laundry and I can feel my hand shaking and they're all looking at me like I'm some pervert and maybe I am, and I'm sure there are a lot of folks who have this kind of stuff, but they don't do stupid things like leave it in the side compartment of their duffel bag.

Then I realize Shin Lee isn't in there. She's the only one who isn't in the room and that's great. At least I don't have to face her. Lucy asks me how I've been and she says it with a big smile on her face but I can't get a clear read if it's a smile like ironic or one of those smiles that you do when you're pissed, and the dad, Joe, is smiling too and they keep going on like this and are taking forever to get my change, and the son, Kim, pulls my duffel bag off the top of a pile in the back, and I'm hanging my head and trying to get the hell out of there before Lucy throws something at me or Joe starts yelling at me. And then the daughter, Shin Lee, comes inside with a big box of detergent and they are all just looking at me and looking at each other and the daughter is blushing and I know my ears are like burning fire red so when I finally get my bag from the teenage boy, Kim, I haul out of there and leave them all talking Chinese to each other, and I'm sure they are just talking about me and saying stuff about all the stuff in the side compartment of my laundry bag.

I know I'm going to have to find a different laundry place, like the guy over on Vanderbilt. And that's what I do, and now when I see the family from By the Pound they ask what happened to me and I mumble something about doing my own wash or whatever. I try to avoid them the best I can but it's hard because their shop is right next to my subway stop and even though I take a roundabout way to get there, even though I walk down up and around to the entrance of the Manhattan bound D train, I do run into them on the block.

I stuff all the freaky stuff in a brown paper bag, and the plan is to shove it in some Dumpster, like the one next to the bodega where Manny and Jesus work, and that's what I do. I get rid of all of it. All the stuff that started this whole thing in the first place.

The other guy, the one over on Vanderbilt who's got a place called "Wash and Fold" doesn't do such a great job of washing and folding and I've found other people's stuff in my wash, like a stray sock and a pair of panties that were the size of a circus tent, and I swear a pair of my favorite jeans have gone missing, and when I ask him about the jeans, the ones that went missing, he shrugs his shoulder and points to a sign that says something about not being responsible for damaged items. That does it, and now I go back to doing my wash myself, which is a real pain in the ass.

My brother asks me why I don't get my wash done by Joe anymore and I tell him I do it myself, like it's something I want to do. I tell him I like to do my own wash. My brother tells me that it takes a whole day doing your wash and you gotta sit in that stupid Laundromat, and when it's all said and done it costs about the same, and I tell him it's no big deal, I tell him it doesn't take me a whole day and I tell him I get work done over there, and my brother shakes his head and tells me that that place, the do-it-yourself Laundromat, is hell with the unruly kids and whatnot, and I agree with him but I don't tell him so.

POSTERS

THIS ONE GUY I KNOW NAMED JARVIS CALLS ME AND ASKS ME IF I WANT TO TAKE OVER THIS JOB THAT HE DOES BECAUSE HE'S GOING HOME TO MILWAUKEE FOR A FEW MONTHS AND HE TELLS ME IT'S A PRETTY SWEET DEAL. Then he tells me he gave this man named Bruce my number and that I should expect a call from him. Bruce calls and he's this guy who lives in Boston and he's got this outfit that puts posters up around the city and he says his outfit is a distribution business and he needs a guy down in the city, and he asks that I might meet him in the city in a couple of days 'cause he has this job for me and he can tell me more about it when I see him.

So I meet this guy Bruce at a café in Chelsea called The Big Drop and it's a place that gay men like to hang out in and I figure this out after I look around the room and I see a man with enormous hairy biceps tongue kiss this other man who had a shaved head and scrawny calves. Bruce seems all right, he's chunky, probably about fifty years old, he's got on jeans and a tan windbreaker and doesn't seem to put much thought into his appearance. He tells me he needs a guy down in the city, and he keeps looking past me and thumbing his thumbs, but not nervous like, more like he likes to thumb his thumbs, and he tells me what I need to do is put up posters, and he asks if I've done this before and I tell him I put up posters for my band all the time, and Bruce doesn't really seem to be listening to what I tell him, he's distracted with something behind me and I don't really care, I just want to find out how much this man pays. He tells me he's got a job for some new kind of liquor and it's a green liquor and it's like five-hundred posters he needs put up and he asks if I'd be interested and I'm like, yeah, definitely. Bruce tells me what I need to do is put the posters up around Manhattan, on street corners, abandoned billboards, lamp posts, and in store fronts, and what he needs me to do is take pictures of the different places where I put them up and the pictures should show where these places are, and he tells me the better the places, the better it is for his business because he gives his clients the pictures of where their posters are put up and they get real excited if it's on Fifth Avenue or Times Square or whatever.

I like this guy Bruce because he pulls out a gang of cash and he peels off five one-hundred dollar bills and he folds the crisp bills in half and his green eyes shift around the room behind me and then he gives a quick look over his left shoulder out the window toward the street and while he's looking the other way he places the money on the table in front of me like this is some high-level transaction, and I'm hoping that this job lasts a long time because this man just paid me in advance for something that he wants done in the future.

I follow Bruce to his white mid-sized rental car and he opens the trunk and there are boxes on top of boxes stacked in the trunk, and he heaves a few boxes out of the trunk and he asks where my car is and I tell him it's nearby and he asks if I want to pull it around and I tell him it's no big deal, I can carry the three boxes to my car - that I actually don't have here because Willie has it with him in Minneapolis. He hands me one of those throwaway cameras and he tells me to take pictures of where I put the posters up and to send him the camera and I'm like, should I get the film developed? And he tells me no, just send the camera.

I lug the boxes into a taxi and tell the driver to take me to Brooklyn. We pull in front of my flat and I slip the driver a one-hundred dollar bill through that slot and he looks at me like I called him a cunt and then asks me what he's supposed to do with this and then he shakes his head and sucks his teeth and drives me over to the bodega on the corner where I buy a six-pack of Heineken and give the guy behind the bullet-proof glass the one-hundred dollar bill, and he writes on the bill with one of them special markers that show whether or not the bill is counterfeit, and I'm pleased when he changes out the hundred-dollar bill with twenties and whatnot.

I cut open one of the boxes and it's for some liquor that is green, and on the poster is a woman who is quite buxom and she's drinking the green liquor and looks to be having a good time and there's some writing beneath her that says something about passion. I pull out a stack of posters and I'm thinking this is going to be a cakewalk. I toss a stack of the posters inside a duffel bag and hoist the duffel bag onto my back, and then I set it back down on the ground and take out about half of the posters. I think about some kind of cart or something on wheels because these fuckers are heavy, and then I get distracted from that thought with the thought of making sure I have my weed, so I go into my room and pinch off some of the Willie weed and I remember that I need to call my dad back.

I go down to the East Village and I find an abandoned building that is all boarded up and the boards are covered with posters for this band or that movie or some kind of booze but they're old and ripped up and I'm thinking I can line the side of the building with the posters of the green liquor and if I get the right angle I can snap a photo that will have the crown of the Empire State Building off in the background. This seems like a really great idea until this man asks me what I'm doing, and this man is pretty disheveled looking but there is something about his sharp eyes and his soiled white high-top sneakers and his three-quarter-length leather coat that puts me a bit on edge and so I hesitate before I tell him I'm putting up posters and I smile at him and he doesn't smile back and I notice he's got some posters too and he's got this mop and a bucket with this goop that looks like snot in it and he's got this method that's all quick and efficient and it's pretty clear he's done this before and he flips up a few posters and his posters are bigger than mine and are for some movie with John Travolta and the posters are bright and colorful and the man with the three-quarter-length leather coat says, not here you're not, and he slaps that snot stuff on the posters with the mop and I realize the snot stuff is glue. Well, that's that because I'm not going to get into it with some guy who puts posters up like that, and I get to thinking that you can't just put stuff up wherever you want, and my idea, the one with the crown of the Empire State Building in the background is not going to happen.

I hoist my bag onto my back and set off farther uptown and those posters with John Travolta on them are all over each and every billboard, and a voice in my head says, poster over all the posters, but clearly that's not going to happen so I head over to the West side and the bag is getting really heavy so I dip inside this bar and order a cold beer.

The guy behind the bar wears a cowboy hat and it's way too big for his head and he doesn't look to be much in the mood for talking, so I open up a stray newspaper on the bar and it's the New York Post and the beer is set in front of me by the cowboy guy and I take a sip and something smells weird so I let the sip go back into the bottle, and something smells dank, like mold or something, and I sniff the beer and then the bottle, and the bottle smells like butt, like it's been sitting in some funky-ass water, so I ask cowboy guy if I could get something else because the bottle smells funny and he says to me, funny? And I'm like yeah, smell it, smell the bottle and he tosses the bottle into a trashcan and it smashes into bits and pieces. I ask what he's got on tap and he doesn't answer me, he just points to a sign that says what kind of beers are on tap and I don't really want the beer anymore and I don't really want to sit here with the cowboy guy.

Then a man comes up behind me and he's fussing with his zipper and his belly hangs out over his belt so he can't see what he's doing and he says something about the newspaper being his, and that kind of does it for me and this establishment, so I hoist the duffel bag onto my shoulder and leave.

I make my way over to Seventh Avenue and I buy a stapler from this man in a hardware store and it's a $16 stapler and I'm thinking that that's a lot of money for a stapler but it's probably a good idea to have one. I staple a poster around a streetlight and I take a picture of it and I do that a few times up and down Seventh Avenue and people look at me and then look at the lady in the poster drinking the green liquor. Then these two kids in oversized denim jackets tell me that I can't put stuff up on their street, and the two kids are those flyer kids who put fluorescent flyers on your car windshield about someone who raps or some club that you'll never go to and they have a gang of posters too and I'm thinking, fuck this, so I decide to wrap this up for the day and I'm thinking what I'll do is take some pictures of these posters some other day.

I walk back down from the way I came and all my posters are ripped down and they are replaced by posters of some rapper whose mouth is open and he's got diamonds on his teeth and he holds a diamond medallion that's bigger than his head, and the poster declares that the new single is in stores now and his name is Diamond and the album and the single are called Diamonds R Forever.

I take solace in the fact that I took some pictures of the posters that were up for ten minutes. I pack a one-hitter of Willie weed and duck inside a phone booth and have a smoke.

I send the camera up to that man Bruce who lives in Boston, and the address he gave me is a post office box and it all seems a bit bizarre. I took a bunch of pictures and I had to be really creative because I discovered a world I didn't know about - it was a world of posters and it was a world where there is territory and you can't just put up posters wherever you want and I put the posters of the lady drinking green liquor up on my street in Brooklyn and I took pictures of them and I made it so you couldn't really see anything distinguishable in the background.

After a few days Bruce calls me and I'm ready to get an earful of dissatisfaction and I'm about to go into my well-rehearsed shpiel about this poster world and the guy with the three-quarter-length leather coat and the hip-hop kids and Diamonds R Forever, when he tells me that I did a great job and he will be back down in the city on Friday and he has another job and he asks if I could maybe get some more people together because this is a bigger job and he tells me there are like a whole gang of posters, so I meet him again at The Big Drop café and he goes through that whole routine with the thumbs and looking over his shoulder and then hands me twenty one-hundred dollar bills and I'm thinking this is a pretty sweet deal.

So after a few months of this business I have piles of boxes of posters for liquors and movies and advertisements stacked on top of stacks out in the hallway of my apartment and now I'm starting to think that I need to get rid of them somehow and my name is printed on the boxes and I need to get rid of the boxes and I need to rip my name off the front of the boxes so I don't get fined or in trouble somehow when I toss the whole lot of them in a Dumpster somewhere out in Brooklyn.

My dad got his $5,000 and Willie's up in Minneapolis with my dad's Turbo Chrysler New Yorker and I have a sack of decent weed under my bed. And sometimes things do work out if you're willing to dump boxes in a dumpster in the middle of the night with two Doberman pinschers hollering their heads off behind a barbed wire fence. I'm praying someone doesn't call the movie or liquor house or whatever and tell them they've found 10,000 posters of their product discarded in Red Hook, Brooklyn. I'm not losing sleep over it. Anyway, I haven't heard from that man Bruce in like six weeks and when I call his number a lady's voice tells me it's been disconnected and I THINK ABOUT THAT THING WHERE PEOPLE SAY ALL GOOD THINGS DO COME TO AN END.

Made in the USA
Lexington, KY
13 May 2012